DATE DUE

SE 11 '98			

DEMCO 38-296

THE EDGE OF THE UNION

THE EDGE OF
THE UNION

THE ULSTER LOYALIST
POLITICAL VISION

Steve Bruce

Oxford University Press
1994

OX2 6DP

Kuala Lumpur Singapore Hong Kong Tokyo
Nairobi Dar es Salaam Cape Town
Melbourne Auckland Madrid
and associated companies in
Berlin Ibadan

Oxford is a trade mark of Oxford University Press

Published in the United States
by Oxford University Press Inc., New York

British Library Cataloguing in Publication Data
Data available

Library of Congress Cataloging in Publication Data
Bruce, Steve, 1954–
The edge of the union: the Ulster loyalist political vision /
Steve Bruce.
Includes bibliographical references and index.
1. Northern Ireland—Politics and government—1969– 2. Violence—
Northern Ireland—History—20th century. I. Title.
DA990.U46B675   1994 941.60824—dc20 94–7710
ISBN 0–19–827975–2—ISBN 0–19–827976–0 (pbk.)

1 3 5 7 9 10 8 6 4 2

Typeset by J&L Composition Ltd., Filey, North Yorkshire
Printed in Great Britain
on acid-free paper by
Biddles Ltd., Guildford and King's Lynn

Preface

FOR the reader who likes to know something of how a book came to be written, I will explain what prompted me to add yet another volume to the depressingly large literature on Northern Ireland. In 1985 I finished writing *God Save Ulster! The Religion and Politics of Paisleyism*, which was, as the title suggests, a study of the church and party founded by Ian Paisley. Six years later I published *The Red Hand*, a sociological study of loyalist paramilitaries. The subjects for those two studies were initially chosen because they had previously been neglected, but later I came to appreciate that, between them, working-class loyalists and the evangelicals who provide the core of Ian Paisley's Democratic Unionist Party represent two major poles in Ulster unionism. Those two books rather improperly earned me the status of Britain's expert on loyalists. With every new political initiative or upsurge in loyalist violence, journalists and media researchers would phone me for the pundit's comment. Flattering though the 'Prods are Me' role was, it increasingly troubled me that there were major questions about the loyalist view of the world for which I could not confidently articulate the answers. As I was pondering the gaps in my understanding, Secretary of State Peter Brooke was promoting another round of political talks, and, though I could not readily identify the weaknesses, I sensed that there was something missing from the British thinking about loyalists.

So that I could be confident that I understood Ulster loyalists, I resolved in 1992 to return to a number of the evangelicals and paramilitaries I had interviewed over the previous decade and ask them how they saw the last twenty-five years (it was twenty-three when I started); how they now saw the political environment; what developments they would like to see; what they feared they would see; what they would tolerate; and what they would find so objectionable that they would be willing to fight to reject it.

As this book will try to elaborate, I found my unease turning into criticism of my own approach. To put it most simply, I feel now that much thinking about Northern Ireland is neither here nor there because it fails to appreciate the strength of ethnic identification, the power of ethnic divisions, and the importance of expressive action. Commentators have too often taken at face value the claims of the various parties to the conflict that what is at issue is individual rights within a stable democratic structure. They have paid too much attention to the surface of conventional politics of agendas, inter-party competition, and position papers. Even allowing for the purple prose and the grainy photographs that are the stock response of the newspapers to every atrocity, the conflict is discussed in the language of modern western European democratic politics when the struggles of Africa or post-Communism eastern Europe would offer better examples.

Before we get to the substance of this book, a few words about the logical status of parts of what follows might save everyone some energy by allowing critics to aim at the right target (if shooting metaphors are not too tasteless in this context). My first concern is to explain what the world looks like to two specific sections of unionism, and, in so far as one can generalize, to unionists at large. For the purposes of understanding those groups, what matters is how they see things, not the underlying reality. The balding man who carefully arranges his few remaining hairs may be quite mistaken in his belief that the effect is flattering but it is none the less that belief which explains why he does it. When, for example, I talk of Protestants' fears of being 'outbred' by Catholics, what matters is not the correctness of their demographic predictions. They are not professional demographers and they may well be wrong. None the less, they act as they do in response to their vision of the world, not to mine. Much of this book (especially the second chapter) is concerned to describe and explain the loyalist view of the world and, in so far as the reader finds elements of that vision distorted, the reader's argument is with Ulster loyalists rather than with me. On a technical point, at various places in the text I use the terms which the people I am describing use to describe themselves and their actions. Partly this is done to give the reader a sense of how the actors see their actions; sometimes it is because there is no single word which is any more accurate. For example, paramilitaries use the term 'operators' to distinguish those members who have been or are prepared to be personally involved in illegal violence from the 'backroom boys', 'armchair generals', and 'politicians'. It should be obvious that I am not offering any personal endorsement of such self-images. It would have been tiresome to surround every such usage with a *cordon sanitaire* of inverted commas, so I have done so only for the first usage.

However, in some places I do wish to evaluate, as well as to illustrate, the views I present, and hence I offer some evidence for or against the loyalist perception. There are three reasons for this. First, the information is interesting in its own right. Secondly, where it shows that the loyalist view is at least plausible, it is a useful corrective to the widespread assumption that unionists are merely paranoid bigots. Thirdly, where it shows that the loyalist view is apparently distorted, it raises interesting questions about why, in this or that matter, loyalist views are so much at odds with those of the disinterested observer.

A final note about the tone of the book: in places the prose is blunt, the assertions dramatic, the sentiments bitter. One reader of an early draft wondered if I was not either exaggerating the depth of feeling or inappropriately generalizing what were the views of only a small number of extremists. It is true that there is no sure way, other than waiting to see how various groups of unionists behave, of knowing how representative are the visions I report here, but there is one reason why my account should be heeded. In Northern Ireland more than in many places, there are two languages spoken. There is what you say in public and in 'mixed' company, and there is what you say in private, among your own people. In public, you make the moderate and guarded statements about 'people round here have always worked together and there has never been any trouble'. In private, you express the hurt and the hatred. A problem for analysis is that most reportage and academic commentary is produced by middle-class people (and the middle class is mixed) or by outsiders whose presence is an invitation to those being researched to present a 'front'. That 'front' may not always be more moderate than the reality—some interviewees enjoy dramatizing their evil—but it will appear more thoughtful and reasoned than the unrehearsed performance. If the people of Northern Ireland were as moderate, tolerant, thoughtful, and forgiving as they often appear in print, there would not have been more than 3,000 dead bodies.

There is a danger in writing about affairs that really are current: one may be overtaken and embarrassed by the turn of events. This book is being completed in the first week of 1994. Six months will have elapsed before it is available in bookshops. It may well be that specific issues which seemed pressing at the time I conducted my interviews will have become yellowing cuttings in a newspaper's morgue by the time this is read. However, the passage of time does offer a useful test of the quality of my insights. If in new and possibly very different circumstances the people I describe here are acting in ways that still make sense, that will be good grounds for taking seriously my explanations.

Acknowledgements

As always, debts have been incurred during this work and I would like to acknowledge them. Small grants from the Economic and Social Research Council funded my travel expenses while I was working on *The Red Hand*. A grant from the British Academy did the same for *God Save Ulster*. The Joseph Rowntree Charitable Trust enabled me to travel to conduct the interviews which form the basis for this book. I would like to thank Stephen Pittam of the Trust for his encouragement in the production of the initial report on which this book is based, Tim Barton and all the staff at Oxford University Press for their assistance in turning a research report into a readable book, but, most importantly, all those people who took the trouble to talk to me.

Contents

1. GUNMEN AND
EVANGELICALS

WHAT in an ideal world do Ulster unionists want? Of all the imaginable futures, which ones are they prepared to swallow? One way of trying to answer those questions, used often enough, is the survey. A random sample of unionists—that is, people who wish to maintain the union between Northern Ireland and Great Britain[1]—is chosen, a list of fixed questions put to them, their answers coded and analysed. There are obvious problems with this. First, our views about complex but important matters can rarely be expressed sensibly by picking one of four choices of answer to a question asked of us by a complete stranger. The prevalence of outdoor toilets is an issue for which surveys are well suited. The feeling of being lost in a world one does not understand is not.

A second feature of surveys is that they treat all respondents as if their views were of equal importance. That is, they investigate the typical, which is fine for those areas of life where the 'typical' is important but not terribly useful in settings where some people are far more insightful or influential than others and where the actions of a few can change the world of many. For these and other reasons, I felt that the clearest sense of unionist thinking would be gained from long unstructured interviews, or, as we social scientists call it, from 'talking to people'. But to whom should I talk?

Though the differences can be exaggerated, Todd makes a useful distinction between Ulster loyalist and Ulster British strands in unionism.[2] To put it very crudely, loyalists are Ulster Protestants first and British second; the Ulster British are British first and only secondarily root their identity in Ulster. Within Ulster loyalism, there are two importantly different worlds: the paramilitary and the evangelical. Though there are rural terrorists and urban evangelicals, those worlds are also largely the urban and the rural. The paramilitaries are thoroughly working class; the evangelicals may be working class or middle class. There is certainly more to loyalism than the gunmen and the born-again Christians, but these two groups can lay claim to vital symbols of Ulster unionism and can exert considerable influence on Protestants beyond their own numbers because they articulate and act out responses which, to a greater or lesser extent, are found in almost all unionists. They do not typify unionism, but they exemplify, in extreme form, beliefs and values that in weaker versions are held by most unionists. The gunmen and the Christians hold positions which will be taken up by a much wider unionist constituency when circumstances press them.

In the next chapter I will describe Northern Ireland through the eyes of my respondents. Here I will explain something of the recent history of the two loyalist constituencies.

THE GUNMEN

Around 1975 the cartoonist Martyn Turner drew a burly working-class loyalist in a tattoo parlour. His right arm was covered in the initials of a bewildering array of paramilitary organizations: UFF, USC, VSC, RHC, PAF. The bespectacled tattooist, trying to find space for a new tattoo, is saying, 'Like the rest of us, young man, you won't be able to take much more of loyalist politics.' There have been many paramilitary groups beginning with 'U' (for 'Ulster'; republican organizations begin with 'I' for 'Ireland'), but most have been very small or have been absorbed by the two main loyalist paramilitary organizations: the Ulster Volunteer Force (UVF) and the Ulster Defence Association (UDA).[3]

The UVF claims descent from the private army created by Sir Edward Carson and Sir James Craig in 1912 to oppose the British government's intention of granting 'home rule' to Ireland. With over 200,000 Protestants joining it, this first UVF was a genuinely mass movement, well trained and well armed, and it had considerable support from the upper classes, in Britain as well as in Ireland.[4] What was set fair for open rebellion was averted by the onset of the First World War. The UVF was enlisted in the British Army as the 36th (Ulster) Division and fought gallantly. Its men died like cattle at the Battle of the Somme. Whether won over by this sacrifice, persuaded by the argument, or coerced by the threat of revolt, the British government accepted the unionist desire to remain British and partitioned the island, allowing twenty-six counties to become the Irish Free State while six of the nine counties of the province of Ulster became 'Northern Ireland'. The region continued to send members to the Westminster Parliament and was bound by Westminster in such matters as defence and foreign policy, but it was given its own parliament (based at Stormont outside Belfast) and a government responsible for most domestic matters, including internal security.

Security was an issue. There was considerable violence in 1920 and 1921 as republicans fought against partition and loyalists fought against republicans. At least 230 people died and there was damage to property worth around £3m. in 1920s prices.[5] Again led by the upper classes, the UVF was revived as a local vigilante movement and again the movement was legitimated by the government, which adopted the UVF units into the Crown forces, this time as a part-time or 'B' element in the Ulster Special Constabulary.

It is often thought that Northern Ireland was at peace from then until 1969. In fact, there were sectarian riots in the 1930s. In 1942 the Irish Republican Army (IRA) killed three police officers and two B Specials. In its campaign from 1957 to 1961, the IRA murdered six Royal Ulster Constabulary (RUC) officers. In 1964 there was rioting in west Belfast after republican Liam McMillan (later Belfast commander of the IRA) stood in a Westminster election. But in these periods there was no great demand for a Protestant vigilante movement, because, though these campaigns reinforced old fears and animosities, few people saw them as a serious threat to the government or to the constitutional position of Northern Ireland. There was widespread confidence in the government's willingness and ability to face terrorism.

The third UVF came to public attention in 1966. Augustus 'Gusty' Spence and a small band of Shankill Road loyalists became the first active group in a shadowy re-creation led by a small number of Unionists unhappy about the political direction of Prime Minister Terence O'Neill, a man who saw himself as a liberal reforming technocrat. In the light of the mayhem of 1970 and 1971, it is hard to see anything in 1966 as justifying fears of a republican coup, but there were portents, for those schooled in reading them. The West Belfast seat at Stormont fell to Gerry Fitt, then standing as a Republican Labour candidate. That year also marked the fiftieth anniversary of the Easter Rising and there were rumours, encouraged by senior officials in the Ulster Unionist Party (UUP), that the Belfast IRA was going to mark the anniversary by taking over the City Hall, just as the first IRA had done with the Post Office in Dublin in 1916.

The UVF murdered three people—a man walking home drunk, an old lady burnt to death by a petrol bomb intended for the pub next door, and a young Catholic barman—and was banned. Thereafter it enjoyed the status of being small, secretive, selective in recruitment, and thoroughly 'military'. Potential recruits were asked if they were prepared to 'go to prison, to kill, or to be killed' for Ulster. Although popular with a small core of the Belfast working class, Spence's team drew little support from the wider Protestant community and was firmly denounced by the middle class and by religious leaders. In an attempt to link Protestant terrorism and Unionist Party unhappiness with O'Neill, Dillon claims that Spence was encouraged and supported by three 'prominent' Unionist politicians, but exaggerates considerably the status of the men involved.[6] What little élite support the UVF enjoyed evaporated as soon as the organization was banned.

Spence lingered in prison, unheeded, from 1966 until 1970. By then the civil-rights marches and protests, government reaction, loyalist responses, interference from London, increasing Catholic violence, and further government over-reaction had fuelled an escalation of conflict that led many working-class Protestants to suppose, in the words that were spray-painted on the walls of the loyalist Shankill Road: 'Gusty was right!' The UVF began to grow and its members started killing again.

What separated the UDA from the UVF was its ambition to be a mass social and political movement. The UDA grew out of a large number of defence groups formed to protect Protestant enclaves of Belfast in the worst of the communal violence of 1970. There was nightly rioting. For six months the IRA planted large bombs inside or outside pubs and clubs used by Protestants or in cars in the centre of Belfast. There were 153 explosions in 1970 and more than 1,000 the following year—almost all of them in Belfast and almost all the work of republicans. The police recorded 213 shooting incidents in 1970. The following year it was 1,756.

In almost all the working-class areas of Belfast, men formed vigilante groups to blockade their streets and keep out the enemy. Each protected a small area, often no more than five or six streets. So there was the Woodvale Defence Association, the Roden Street Defenders, the Hammer Defence Association, and so on. And there were the big ones: the Shankill Defence Association and the East Belfast Defence Association. These were genuinely popular organizations, often recruiting most of the able-bodied young men of an area. But it is worth noting just who felt threatened this time. In 1912 and 1920 all classes of Ulster Protestants supported vigilante action because they believed that something valued by all Ulster Protestants was at risk. In 1970 only the working classes were so stirred.[7]

In part this represented a change in identity. The aristocracy that provided the officer corps and the training grounds for the first two UVFs had in the intervening years migrated to England or withdrawn from any aspect of public life more controversial than charity work. Much of the middle class had smoothed down its unionism with the modernizing rhetoric of Terence O'Neill and then, like the aristocracy, responded to his demise by abandoning the public world for the certainties of the family hearth. And the middle-class hearths were not in the streets that were being petrol-bombed.

The UDA was formed out of the various local associations in

the summer of 1971 and grew rapidly, so that it could soon turn three or four thousand uniformed and marching men on to the streets. Although its public leaders maintained that the UDA was defensive, there were from the start members who thought the best form of defence was attack. The thinking was simple. The 'Taigs' had already got three-quarters of the island in 1920 and they were not going to get Ulster. The IRA is killing Prods; we will kill republicans. If we cannot find republicans, we will kill Catholics. If we are as vicious as the IRA, we will hamper its operations, punish the Catholic community for its support of the IRA, and make sure that the British government does not have only one source of violence to placate. So that the UDA was not banned like the UVF, its 'operators' claimed their murders under the *nom de guerre* of the Ulster Freedom Fighters (UFF), a name that, with its suggestions of seeking liberation from an imperialist power, was chosen as a joke.

The UDA and UVF responded to IRA violence with mounting enthusiasm. In 1970 the IRA killed eighteen people; loyalists killed two. In 1971 the IRA killed ninety-three people; the Protestants killed twenty-one.

Reactive Violence

The word 'responded' is used deliberately. Not surprisingly, every party wishes to present its crimes as a reasonable response to the vile deeds of the other side; 'they started it!' may seem childish, but it will usually do to make people feel better about their own sins. There has been much debate about the relationship between republican and loyalist violence. The commonly made assertion that loyalists' murder is 'counter-terrorism' provokes strong reactions.[8] It is held that to describe loyalist murder as 'reactive' is factually inaccurate, morally offensive, and politically dangerous. The second and third points are important, but readers may strike their own postures on those issues without my prompting. What I want to do is address and untangle some of the complexities that surround the factual question.

A preliminary problem is that we are taking together individual acts and group rates. Strictly speaking, it makes little sense to talk about 'loyalist violence' (or republican violence, for that matter) as if it were a unitary thing, like 'Fred's violence'. In the case of a single individual, we can settle the issue by looking at the causal sequence of who hit whom first and we can enquire after the motives of the two people. If Fred only hit Jim after Jim had hit Fred and Fred says that he did so because Jim hit him, that would be grounds for describing what Fred did as reactive. But when you are talking about the separate actions of hundreds of people, even when there is a degree of co-ordination in those acts, it is much harder to use the term for anything other than cheap political point-scoring.

We can look at the causal sequence. But as soon as one asks which side struck the first blow, one begins to appreciate that there are at least three other questions hidden in that one: at whom was the first blow struck; which side struck the first blow serious enough to warrant retaliation; and which side first threatened the status quo and thus created reasonable fears of future violence?

But first one has to decide when to start the counting. For every suggested starting date, someone can suggest an earlier atrocity that justified that act, and so on in infinite regress. Thus the 1970 IRA could justify attacks on loyalists by pointing out that the 1966 UVF killed three people (one by accident). But the 1966 UVF justified its actions by referring back to the IRA campaign of the 1950s. Republicans could justify that campaign by pointing to loyalist violence in the 1920s, and so on back to 1690 and to Cromwell.

If we follow convention and take the civil-rights demonstrations in 1969 as the start of the present conflict, we might want to agree with Father Joseph McVeigh, who asserts: 'Although many have been killed in the conflict over the past 20 years, the early deaths and bombings were caused by the British army and their loyalist allies, not by republican forces'.[9] This is at the same time minimally true and misleading. The loyalist bombs of 1969 were either small token devices or were used to damage remote public utilities. They were not attacks on people, and the only person who died was a bomber who electrocuted himself while planting the devices. They were thus quite different from the bombs planted by the IRA in 1971. In May of that year drinkers in the Mountainview Tavern on the Shankill Road were seriously injured by an IRA bomb. A large IRA bomb went off at the British Legion Club in Suffolk. In September two men were killed and twenty injured in an IRA bomb attack on the Four Step Inn on the Shankill. There were many more before the UVF planted a bomb in McGurk's Bar in December and killed fifteen people.[10]

As for McVeigh's view that the early deaths were 'caused by the British army and their loyalist allies', one has to be very cautious. First, it is poor history to see the British army at this stage as an ally of the loyalists. However one interprets their later actions, initially the troops were seen as protecting Catholic areas from Protestant attacks. Their presence was certainly read by many loyalists as unwarranted interference by London in the affairs of Northern Ireland. Secondly, the early deaths of the Troubles shared a common characteristic that distinguished them from most of what was to follow: most occurred in circumstances of disorder, much of it deliberately stimulated in order to provoke the government into over-reacting and thus to further mobilize anti-state sentiment. Of the thirteen people who were killed in the first year, two were Protestants shot by republicans during communal rioting and one was a Catholic shot by a loyalist sniper in similar circumstances. Two were Protestants shot by the army during rioting on the Shankill Road. Earlier in the same disturbances, an RUC constable had been shot by loyalists. The remaining seven were all killed by the RUC or B Specials. One and possibly two were complete accidents. With one exception, the other victims were killed during riots and demonstrations. The security forces doubtless explained their acts as reasonable force and, with two Protestant victims, could claim a certain even-handedness. Critics could see the police use of fatal force as evidence that the police were such callous bastards that they deserved to die. This is a reasoned position, but it is significantly less attractive than the one implied by McVeigh, who, by failing to distinguish between the circumstances in which people were killed in different phases of the conflict, makes one set of actions look like another set which was arguably very different.

I raise the question of the severity of retaliation because clearly the notion of reaction implies appropriate reaction rather than over-reaction. Shooting dead a man who stabs you would probably be accepted as reasonable by most people; shooting dead a man who slapped or insulted you would not. The parallel in communal violence is not easy to draw because we are not only comparing single acts for severity but also considering the cumulative effect. How much persistent abuse warrants shooting dead a policeman?

Although most of the people to whom I talked who had become involved in terrorism could point to some specific atrocity committed by the other side as justification, I suspect that a single cause was unnecessary. Each side holds such negative views of the other that, even if 'the bastards' are not trying to kill you this week or this year, it is only because they are regrouping after the last effort and will be back with more soon. Peace and harmony are never seen as the natural condition, only as a lull in the continuing oppression or rebellion (depending on which side you are on). The abiding expectation of more trouble to come explains why people went so quickly from fighting in the street to murder. The very rapid escalation of violence in August 1969 and the speed with which guns replaced bricks demonstrate that working-class Catholics and Protestants were so thoroughly primed to attack each other that who threw the first brick and fired the first shot is almost certainly accidental—a matter of resources rather than desires. However, if one has to construct an ordered sequence of events, it would be as follows: the UVF's timid and ineffectual campaign of 1966, Catholic-led public disorder in 1969, security-force reaction to that disorder, more Catholic and Protestant disorder, and then the assassination campaign, with republicans being well in the lead of loyalists. That republicans were the first to engage in deliberate and large-scale murder is clear from the table and figure in the Appendix at the end of this book.

One final thought may be useful to move us beyond asking who started the killing to thinking how it might end. There is

clearly a difference between republican and loyalist violence in
its declared purposes and hence in what conditions would cause it
to cease. There should be general agreement about the following
reasoning. If there was no further threat to the constitutional
status of Northern Ireland, a small number of loyalists would
continue to murder but the vast majority would cease (and there
is evidence for that in the sharp decline in loyalist murders in
1978-85). However, if there was a cessation of loyalist violence,
an end to actions by the security forces that went beyond self-
defence, and a severity of social control such as accepted in, say,
Scotland, would the IRA cease its offensive? Some IRA men
would, but, as republican terror has an aim other than
retaliation—the political goal of ending the partition of
Ireland—then one has to presume it would not stop. While the
desire of Catholics for revenge on the UDA and UVF puts some
pressure on the IRA, the main purpose of republican violence is
to effect a particular political change, and whether the IRA
continues to murder or ceases will depend far more on republican
thinking about the likelihood of forcing constitutional change
than on the actions of loyalists. Or, to phrase the difference
another way, if there had been no uprising against the status quo
ante 1969, there would not be the present loyalist terror, but, if
there had been no UDA or UVF, there would still be the IRA.

In the triangular pattern of conflict, the war between
republicans and the security forces was the one that attracted
most attention. This is not to say that loyalists got away with it. It
is nationalists who each year mark the anniversary of the
introduction of internment without trial, but leading loyalist
paramilitaries were also interned. With the exception of curfew,
every reduction of civil liberties introduced to control republicans
was also applied to loyalists. Because it was more furtive, the
UVF was less easy to police than the UDA/UFF, whose members
were surprisingly blatant about their murders—so much so that,
though the police had trouble finding evidence for criminal
charges that would stick, they were able to identify and intern, or
hold on repeated and long periods of remand, many of the main
operators. Yet loyalist murders did not have a political impact on
the same scale as republican ones. Partly this was because the

British media were more interested in attacks on 'our lads' than in those on Catholics. Partly it was because, in the general context of the times, single bodies here and there—the consequences of the typical loyalist operation—did not stick in the general public's memory as long as the big car bombs that were then the stock-in-trade of the IRA. But there is the point that there was genuine uncertainty about which organization was responsible for many of the murders between 1972 and 1975, and doubt allowed everyone to blame many unattributed cases on the other side and thus lessen their awareness of the extent to which their own side was 'stiffing' people.[11] For example, the papers initially described the UVF's bombing of McGurk's Bar as an IRA own goal, and by the time the truth was being widely reported there had been sufficient fresh outrages to allow people who were at all sympathetic to the loyalist paramilitaries to forget that incident.

In the early 1970s the loyalist paramilitaries effectively maintained three different faces. There was the almost respectable community action and political face, illustrated, for example, by Tommy Herron, the leader of the UDA in east Belfast, standing for election as a candidate for the Vanguard Unionist Party. Then there was the disciplined marching uniformed body which claimed to be defensive but which was intended to represent the threat of highly selective and controlled retaliation. This was the UDA on parade or the UVF as it was depicted by Gusty Spence writing from the compounds in the Maze internment camp. And beneath that image there were the murder gangs, sometimes murdering republican activists but more often than not just 'stiffing a taig', groups of men, their resentment often fuelled by long hours drinking in bars, who decided to 'fuckin' well do something'.

The Executive and the Strike

One might describe 1974 as the most successful year for the loyalist paramilitaries in that they managed to operate on all three fronts without performance in one undermining the credibility of the others. In a scheme which set the precedent for producing imaginative initiatives without consulting unionists, in 1973 the British government, like a conjuror drawing a dove from his sleeve, announced the resolution to the conflict: a new form of devolved government in which executive positions would be divided between liberal unionists and the nationalist Social Democratic and Labour Party (SDLP). Because they had already announced that they would not accept a scheme which guaranteed power to the nationalist SDLP irrespective of its vote, conservative unionists were not invited to Sunningdale, where the final details of the agreement were resolved. The scheme created a 'power-sharing' executive, with Brian Faulkner, the leader of the UUP, and last Prime Minister of the old Stormont, as chief executive and Gerry Fitt, the leader of the SDLP, as his deputy. Other Executive posts were divided between those unionists willing to serve, the SDLP, and the small middle-of-the-road Alliance Party. The concession to the SDLP for its involvement in the government of the six counties was the creation of an inter-governmental Council of Ireland, which would allow the British, Irish, and Northern Irish governments to discuss matters of mutual interest and which could, should the majority ever wish it, be the framework for the future unification of Ireland. This the SDLP could present to its supporters as implicit recognition of the legitimacy of nationalist aspirations.

The pro-Executive side had a majority in the Assembly. The once monolithic UUP was split. We cannot be entirely sure which UUP candidates supported Faulkner, but he probably had twenty-two members, while the SDLP had nineteen and the Alliance Party had eight. Firmly opposed to institutional power-sharing were eight Ulster Unionists, eight members of Paisley's Democratic Unionist Party (DUP), seven supporters of Bill Craig's Vanguard (a right-wing Unionist ginger group then in the process of becoming a party), and three independent unionists.[12]

The Executive took office on New Year's Day 1974 but only two months later had its legitimacy fatally undermined by the unfortunate timing of a Westminster general election. Ironically, this election was called by the Conservative Prime Minister Edward Heath to dramatize his claim that the country was being held to ransom by militant trade unionists. He gave the people an opportunity to decide who ran the country, by which he meant Great Britain. In so doing he laid the foundations that allowed the Protestant working class in Northern Ireland to show the government who ran its country.

Had the groups in favour of power-sharing—the liberal Unionists, the Alliance, and the SDLP—been sufficiently committed to it to form a coalition and ask the electorate for a mandate for their experiment, they might have maintained the momentum of the Executive. Instead they competed against each other. The anti-power-sharing parties presented a common front by running just one candidate in each constituency and won eleven of the twelve seats. Worse, the anti-power-sharing parties took 51 per cent of the vote, while the parties supporting Faulkner gained only 41 per cent. Worse still, only 13 per cent of unionist votes went to Faulkner's liberals. Unionists were the majority in Northern Ireland and a majority of them were opposed to Sunningdale.

With their election victory as justification, the opponents of Sunningdale decided to try direct action. Despite their fiery rhetoric, the politicians were clearly reluctant to press civil disobedience, and the leaders of key groups of workers and of the paramilitary organizations had to present Bill Craig of Vanguard, Harry West for the conservative part of the UUP, and Paisley for the DUP with a *fait accompli*. With Glen Barr, who was active in the trade-union movement and in Vanguard as well as being the main strategist for the UDA, in the chair of the organizing committee, the Ulster Workers' Council (UWC) called a general strike.

The strike began on 15 June and, to the surprise of almost everyone, took only fourteen days to force the Executive to resign. Crucial to the success were the power-workers, who were tacitly supported by the middle management of the power-generating stations and who quickly brought the province grinding to a halt. The loyalist paramilitaries provided road blocks and intimidation, but the gradual run-down of power supplies meant that even those people who did get to work found there was little for them to do. The strikers managed to close the port of Larne and prevent the movement of agricultural supplies and Protestant farmers blocked roads with their tractors. In working-class areas of Belfast the paramilitaries arranged for the delivery of essential food supplies and re-created something of the blitz spirit, as residents of Protestant communities bravely put up with the inconveniences by pulling together in their common goal.

The conspiracy theorists of the Northern Ireland conflict (almost as numerous and as bizarre as the students of the Kennedy assassination) believe that the British security forces encouraged the strike to bring down the Sunningdale agreement. Yorkshire Television's *First Tuesday* programme even went so far as to suggest that the UVF bombs which killed twenty-seven people in Dublin and Monaghan town during the strike were the work of the SAS.[13] Quite why a section of the British establishment should want further to destabilize Northern Ireland is not explained, but that unfortunately popular line of thinking does the major disservice of belittling unionist unhappiness with the Sunningdale agreement. By suggesting that *agents provocateurs* were needed to provoke the strike,[14] it misses the point that a very wide section of unionism saw Sunningdale as a major weakening of the Union with Britain and was either anxious to oppose it or, once others had started the opposition, was quite happy to do nothing to save the Executive. To appreciate why even middle-class unionists were willing to destroy what with hindsight is seen by many to have been the last chance to retain devolved government in the province, it has to be remembered that the SDLP leaders who were now given government office were the people who had led the civil-rights campaign and who had frequently declared their intention to destroy the constitutional status of Northern Ireland. To introduce a theme which will recur throughout this book, unionists were not consoled by the claim that the SDLP, by accepting office, was abandoning its nationalist agenda. They supposed that this was not a final deal but only a temporary accommodation which would be followed in time by a further escalation of nationalist demands.

Although the definitive history of the strike has yet to be written, it is clear that the UDA played a major part in co-ordinating the strike. Barr and the other paramilitary leaders hoped to be able to turn their muscle into positive power but found that the successful end of the strike was also the end of their political clout. A common purpose among the paramilitaries was soon replaced by arguments amongst themselves about what they should do next. Ironically, by bringing to an end the exercise in devolved government, the strikers removed a vital forum for local political activity. Once again, the running of the province was firmly in the hands of politicians and civil servants from London; such political authority as there was now belonged only to the main political parties who had representatives at Westminster, and the paramilitaries were excluded.

The Doldrums and the Revival

The late 1970s saw a gradual but real improvement in the security situation, as the reorganized RUC began to enjoy more success in controlling the terrorists. Many UDA men came to the conclusion that they had served their purpose by forcing a more robust security response to republicanism and stood down. So long as the UDA was more than just a terrorist organization, the government saw some value in going along with the fiction that the UFF was not just the UDA with a different code word. So long as the leaders of the UDA had an agenda other than terrorism, they had reason to restrain their more violent members. The initiative within the organization passed to those people with political ambitions, and for a decade from 1978, while the UDA promoted various political initiatives (which in the end proved fruitless), no year saw more than three UDA/UFF murders.

From their inception, the loyalist paramilitaries had funded themselves by robberies and extortion, but, so long as the political climate was tense enough for many people to support their murder campaigns, there was little criticism of racketeering, which could be tolerated as a necessary evil. Though anyone involved in or on the fringes of the UDA must have known that leaders such as Tommy Herron and Charles Harding Smith were engaged in crimes which enriched them as well as the organization, many accepted that they were also doing a 'decent job'. However, the long period of relative inactivity in the 1980s saw increasing attention to gangsterism and the gradual build-up of criticism from the community and pressure for action from the lower ranks. The signing of the Anglo-Irish accord in 1985 (of which more later) further increased unhappiness about UDA inertia. In 1987, made slack by years in power, the old guard began to tumble. Reports of the building-site extortion rackets of Jimmy Craig had become commonplace. Only the intimidation of witnesses prevented his conviction. In August one brigadier was filmed trying to extort protection money from TV journalist Roger Cook.[15] Four months later John McMichael, who combined the roles of military commander and political spokesman, was murdered by the IRA, allegedly aided by information from a senior UDA man. Two weeks later another brigadier was arrested while shifting a large consignment of weapons. These failures added to the swell of criticism of the leadership of Andy Tyrie, Supreme Commander for sixteen years. At a heated meeting of commanders, Tyrie responded to the criticism by resigning. The remaining brigadiers from the 1970s had only a year in charge before they fell foul of their own desire to prove that their organization was not engaged in a campaign of murder against randomly selected Catholics. In defending their murder of Loughlin Maginn, they produced copies of security-force documents which described him as an IRA suspect. Although there are conspiracy thinkers who believe that traitors within the UDA's leadership deliberately provoked the hostile response and brought down on their heads the Stevens inquiry into collusion between security forces and the UDA, it is more likely that the leaders simply miscalculated the impact of their very public demonstration that they possessed intelligence information that had come from security-force sources.

The result of the Stevens inquiry was double-edged: a lot of senior UDA men spent 1990 in prison, but the army lost Brian Nelson, its spy in the UDA, which gave new confidence to the UFF element that it could now act unmonitored and unrestrained.

To re-establish the organization's credibility, the new leaders promised an internal purge and, in October 1989, had Jimmy Craig killed, allegedly for racketeering and for aiding republicans

to assassinate leading loyalists. Then in 1991, after the joint
UVF–UDA cease-fire called during Peter Brooke's constitutional
talks, the UFF started a murder campaign that saw as many
victims in eighteen months as in the whole of the 1980s. In
August 1992 the government banned the UDA and thus set it on a
par with the UVF, which has continued since its inception to
practise terror.

It is not much of an exaggeration to say that the wholesale
clear-out of the UDA's top ranks and its proscription produced
the opposite of the intended effect. The Nelson fiasco led to a
major reorganization. Borrowing from the model of the IRA, the
UFF created a series of small cells. The flow of intelligence to the
security forces dried up. With the restraining influences gone, the
operators were able to step up their murder campaign. In addition
to the usual easy targets of Catholic taxi-drivers and Catholic
families living on the fringes of Protestant areas, the UFF
murdered a number of Sinn Fein activists.

Journalists, when they list a number of victims, often divide
them into categories and weigh the number of arguably legitimate
against the sectarian murders, but I suspect that people who are
not resolutely opposed to loyalist terror follow a more
sympathetic line of reasoning which involves easily forgetting
the taxi-drivers and remembering the one or two high-profile
targets. Between 1989 and 1992 there were enough of those for
perceptions of the organization to change quite considerably in
working-class areas. Though the politicians and church leaders
continued to criticize the gunmen, more and more young men
volunteered. As a UDA leader put it: 'The banning of our
organization was wrong. It was a sop to the SDLP and the Dublin
government. Though having said that, the effect, in real terms,
has been an upsurge in people applying to join and also a
recognisable rise in the quality of new recruit.[16] The additional
personnel and more sympathetic climate meant that, despite
police success in arresting a number of murder squads, the killing
continued to escalate.

It is extremely difficult to estimate the size and popularity of
the two main loyalist paramilitary organizations. What is clear,
however, is that, though the UDA has lost the status it once had

as a mass movement, in its new more narrowly terrorist role it has regained a considerable degree of support from the male urban working-class young. The unanimous verdict of commentators is that since 1990 there have been hundreds of new recruits, especially in the working-class estates of Belfast. A teacher in a state school in west Belfast asked a class of 7-year-olds what they wanted to be when they grew up. One boy said: 'A UDA man!' His friend, displaying more ambition, said: 'A UDA brigadier.'

Unlike that of the UDA, the leadership of the smaller UVF has remained relatively stable. There was some disruption in the early 1980s when a number of highly publicized trials saw large numbers of alleged UVF men held on remand for long periods and convicted on the uncorroborated testimony of three 'supergrasses'. Almost all were later released when, on appeal, the supergrass testimony was judged to be unreliable. There was a marked decline in the popularity of the organization in the late 1970s when the 'team' led by Murphy, Bates, and Moore—the infamous 'Shankill Butchers'—was convicted for nineteen murders, many of them lingering deaths inflicted with knives and hatchets. But, though specific features of the UVF explain some changes in its fortunes, the pattern of violence followed a similar trajectory to that of the UDA. In the mid-1970s the UVF's murder rate dropped dramatically. It was slightly more active than the UDA (especially in the mid-Ulster area) through the 1980s and, as the UDA became more active at the end of the decade, so too did the UVF, albeit at a lower level.

THE EVANGELICALS

Ian Paisley is almost certainly unique in twentieth-century European politics in having founded both an enduring religious organization and a successful political party, and the rarity of that combination should alert us to what is often ignored: the vital part that religion plays in Protestant politics. From his teenage years, Paisley had been a virulent critic of liberalism both in Ulster religion (which primarily means within the Presbyterian Church of Ireland, the largest Protestant denomination in Ulster) and in unionist politics (which means within the UUP). Because the primary political issue in Ulster followed the divisions of ethnic identity, which in turn followed the fault line of the Reformation, the enemy in both religion and politics was the same: those who would compromise with Rome. For the young Paisley the compromisers in the Presbyterian Church and the liberals in the UUP were both set on the Romeward trend.

In 1951 dissident Presbyterians in Crossgar joined themselves to Paisley's own independent congregation in east Belfast to form the Free Presbyterian Church of Ulster, which grew only very slowly until the last years of the 1960s, when incipient political instability gave a new significance to his claims that the Irish Presbyterian Church was compromising the historic evangelical doctrines.[17] That the growth of Free Presbyterianism was related to Protestants' increasing sense of unease about political developments can be seen from the pattern of church-planting. Only twelve congregations were founded between 1951 and 1965 (and one of these folded). Twenty-two were added in the five years between 1966 and 1971. The following decade saw another fifteen founded. The church now numbers some 12,000 people, which makes it the fourth largest Protestant denomination in Northern Ireland.

Just as Paisley's theological ultra-orthodoxy had limited appeal until the political climate appeared to confirm his claims about the consequences of liberalism, so his persistent criticisms of the UUP drew little attention or support until the civil-rights movement appeared to confirm his claim that to placate the demands of nationalists would only encourage them to become more demanding.

In 1966 Paisley formed the Ulster Constitution Defence Committee (UCDC) as a vehicle for his political protests. One of his supporters, Noel Doherty, organized the Ulster Protestant Volunteers (UPV) as the rank-and-file movement of the Committee; the name was deliberately chosen to remind people of the 1912 Ulster Volunteer Force. Although there is no evidence that Paisley planned or encouraged violence (he was quick in his public condemnation of the UVF men who killed Peter Ward in Malvern Street in 1966), a number of UPV men were also in Spence's UVF and they chose to give substance to their claims of a resurgent IRA by playing the IRA's part and blowing up a variety of public-service installations. In March and April 1969 they bombed an electricity substation at Castlereagh and the Silent Valley reservoir in the Mournes. The links between the UPV and UVF were exposed when Thomas McDowell, a member of the Kilkeel Free Presbyterian Church, was burnt to death while trying to bomb an electricity substation across the border in County Donegal.[18]

In 1969 Paisley felt confident enough of support for his criticism of Premier Terence O'Neill to contest O'Neill's seat in the Stormont parliament for the Bannside constituency of North Antrim, the farming heartland of rural evangelicals. Standing as a Protestant Unionist, Paisley took 24 per cent of the vote to the Prime Minister's 29 per cent. More damaging perhaps, one of Paisley's student ministers managed to take 33 per cent of the vote in South Antrim. O'Neill resigned shortly after and Paisley won the Stormont seat at a by-election in April 1970. He then built on that momentum by contesting the Westminster constituency that included the Stormont area of Bannside in June 1970 and won it with 41 per cent of the vote. The violence and political instability of the two previous years had taken Ian Paisley from being a Jeremiah crying in the wilderness to a seat at the centre of British politics.

Throughout the summer of 1971 Paisley held meetings with right-wingers within the UUP and appeared to be promised considerable support for creating an alternative to the now suspect Unionist Party, but in the event, when he launched the Ulster Democratic Unionist Party (DUP) in October 1971 with the intention of broadening his base from the rural evangelicals who had been the mainstay of the Protestant UUP, he found that many right-wingers preferred to remain with the Unionists. Parts of the 'secular' right wing came out to form Vanguard, and for a period there were four unionist parties: Paisley's DUP, the Vanguard led by former Minister for Home Affairs William Craig, the right wing within the UUP (which because it controlled most of the party's branches called itself the Official Unionist Party or OUP), and the liberal unionists led by Brian

Faulkner. By the end of the 1970s, this had simplified to just two as the right wing regained control of the UUP and Vanguard folded.

The electoral fortunes of the DUP have since risen and fallen, mostly in relation to the opportunities for local politics and the fact of unionist coalitions. Because it is the bigger party and Westminster elections are fought on a 'winner-takes-all' voting system, the UUP has always had more parliamentary seats than the DUP, and, on the occasions that the two unionist parties have felt that a common front is required, the agreement not to field candidates against incumbents of the other party has consolidated the UUP's primacy and prevented the DUP from advertising its more aggressively resolute unionism. When there have been local assemblies or constitutional conventions and when it has been free to criticize the UUP for actual or potential liberal deviations, the DUP has done well, and at local government elections it has come close to the UUP. Indeed in 1982 it gained more first-preference votes.

Paisley himself has prospered politically even more than his party. The decision to treat Northern Ireland as a single constituency with three seats for the European Community parliament created a province-wide popularity contest, and Paisley has easily won that contest on every occasion. In 1979 Paisley gained 29 per cent of the first-preference votes (as compared to 25 per cent for John Hume of the constitutional nationalist SDLP and 22 per cent for the two UUP candidates). In 1984 he increased his first-preference vote to a full third of all Ulster voters (over 230,000) and repeated the performance five years later.

To summarize, though Paisley's religious and political movements were founded in anticipation of the present Troubles and were initially thought to be of little account, the instability has seen them grow to represent major constituencies within the religious and political life of the province. Furthermore, by being available as a home for dissidents from the Irish Presbyterian Church and the UUP, the movements have acted to retard liberal tendencies in those organizations and have thus exerted an influence way beyond the reach of their membership.

POLITICS AND RELIGION

What needs to be stressed is that, for Northern Ireland loyalists, politics and religion are connected. The connection is complex. In *God Save Ulster*, I began my explanation of the role of religion with the dramatic assertion that 'the Northern Ireland conflict is a religious conflict'.[19] Though the subsequent argument detailed exactly what I meant by that, a number of authors have misunderstood my point. O'Duffy, for example, suggests that I see 'the conflict primarily as a religious war, as a relic of the Reformation/Counter-reformation struggle'.[20] Such a summary is actually a long way from my point.

There are in Northern Ireland Protestants who see all history as a struggle between the forces of good and evil, God and the Devil, Christ and the Anti-Christ. They interpret the republican and nationalist causes as part of a continuing campaign by the Roman Catholic Church to undermine those countries and erode those populations which most strongly support the Reformed Protestant faith. Paisley is one such person. In Northern Ireland there are more people than there are anywhere else in the Western world who see the hidden hand of Rome behind all social and political evils. But they remain a minority—perhaps no more than 15 per cent of the population.

What is fascinating about Paisley's influence is not that most members of his small denomination support his politics but that very large numbers of people outside the conservative evangelical world of gospel halls and revival meetings also support him. What I want to draw attention to is the part that evangelical religion plays in the ethnic identity of Ulster loyalists.

First, let me establish the point that needs explaining by showing the considerable extent to which evangelicalism permeates loyalist politics. In his early days Paisley drew heavily on his 'home boys' in the Free Presbyterian Church of Ulster. In 1969, of six Protestant Unionist election candidates, three were Free Presbyterian (FP) ministers and one was an FP elder. The rapid growth of the party did not see evangelical representation reduced. I was able to identify the denomination of some 400 DUP candidates who stood in a variety of elections (local council, assembly, or convention) between 1972 and 1980. Only some 1 per cent of people in Northern Ireland who are not Roman Catholic belong to the Free Presbyterian Church but, for the sample of six different groups of DUP activists, an average of 64 per cent are Free Presbyterians. Even more striking, most of those who were not FP were members of other conservative evangelical denominations. The three main denominations—the Irish Presbyterian Church, the Church of Ireland, and the Methodists—are all greatly under-represented. As if the evangelicalism of the DUP were not sufficiently attested to by these figures, many of the Irish Presbyterians and Baptists seemed almost obliged to apologize for not having abandoned apostate denominations. They signified their place on the evangelical wing of their churches by adding to their election literature that they were 'evangelical', 'involved in mission work', or some such reference.

Yet we know from the sheer size of the DUP vote that the vast majority of DUP voters are not evangelicals. One must conclude that they like being represented by evangelicals. Of course, this may have nothing to do with religion. Non-believers might support evangelicals because they believe them to be dogmatic and doctrinaire, and hence more reliably unionist than people in the other unionist parties. There is doubtless an element of this. However, the unionist electorate has in the past been presented with non-evangelical political representatives who were every bit as resolute in their unionism as the 'God botherers'. In the 1975 Convention elections, for example, the Vanguard Party fielded a number of loyalist candidates, some of them paramilitary figures well known in their areas. They did less well than the DUP evangelicals, and when their votes were transferred they often went, not to another Vanguard member, but to the DUP candidate. The relative unpopularity of loyalist candidates, even before some of them flirted with such dangerous political innovations as voluntary coalition, socialism, or independence, suggests that non-evangelical support for evangelicals is not completely or even largely explained by the voters' knowledge that Free Presbyterians are extremists.

It is also worth noting that DUP activists do not disguise their religious commitments. The election literature of many candidates goes out of its way to stress their religious probity, and, once in office, DUP councillors have often pursued their temperance and Sabbath-keeping principles even when it was clear that their actions (in, for example, closing leisure facilities on Sundays) were not popular.

Paisley himself is not a politician who just happens to be a clergyman; he is a politician who makes no bones about his religious calling and who puts religious orthodoxy above political advantage. To give just one recent example, in January 1986 all the unionist Members of Parliament resigned their seats so that they could use the resulting by-elections to demonstrate against the Anglo-Irish accord signed the previous November. The unionist leaders knew it was vital to maximize the unionist vote, and Paisley and James Molyneaux (the leader of the UUP) put considerable effort into presenting a united front. But on the eve of the elections Paisley's daughter and a number of his ministers attended and tried to disrupt an ecumenical service organized by the Church of Ireland in St Anne's Cathedral in Belfast. The night before he wanted to maximize the unionist vote, Paisley was willing to allow his religious followers to annoy Church of Ireland Protestants.

It is also worth stressing that the connection between evangelicalism and unionism goes beyond the linking of the two in the biography and ideology of Ian Paisley. In the rural Presbyterian heartlands of Ulster (the Roe Valley, for example), there seems almost nothing to separate an Irish Presbyterian member of the Orange Order who votes Ulster Unionist from an FP member of the Independent Orange Order (Paisley's alternative fraternal organization) who votes Democratic Unionist, except the view of Paisley. When the Irish Presbyterian minister of Limavady made a number of highly charged fraternal gestures towards the local Catholic priest, the Free Presbyterians picketed David Armstrong's church, but it was his own congregation which forced him out.[21]

In 1985 the Ulster Clubs movement was launched, initially by working-class loyalists in Portadown. The UDA was involved in the Clubs, but they have also recruited DUP and UUP supporters. At first sight, it might seem that the Clubs represented a working-class alternative to the DUP, which, although it has strong working-class support, is predominantly a 'respectable' bourgeois organization with its base among small farmers. We might have expected religious elements to be absent from the rhetoric and activities of the Ulster Clubs, but this was not the case. The leader, Alan Wright, was a convinced Salvation Army evangelical who saw the fight against nationalism as a religious struggle: 'at the end of the day my politics are not divisible from my faith. It's Protestantism versus Rome.' When he retired from the Clubs, he announced his intention to go to Bible college. Although many of the supporters of the late George Seawright, a North Belfast loyalist councillor expelled from the DUP, were 'non-religious' Protestants, the core of his small Ulster Protestant League was evangelical. Seawright was himself an elder in the Free Presbyterian Church before moving to the Church of God, where he acted as a lay preacher.

One final illustration will make the point. In 1981 there was a by-election in the South Belfast constituency; the sitting UUP member had been murdered by the IRA. The Revd Robert Bradford had shifted from the mainstream Methodists to the Independent Methodists because the former were insufficiently evangelical.[22] His seat was contested by, for the DUP, the FP Revd William McCrea and, for the UUP, the Revd Martin Smyth, a Presbyterian minister on the evangelical wing of his church and Grand Master of the Orange Order.

If we accept that evangelical Protestantism resonates with Ulster unionists far beyond the small core of evangelicals, how can we explain such resonance? The key point is the centrality of evangelicalism for the Ulster loyalist's sense of ethnic identity. It defines the group to which he belongs, it figures large in the history of that group, it legitimates the group's advantages (such as they are), and it radically distinguishes the group from its traditional enemy.

First, we have history. Religion was already an important source of social divisions at the point of settlement. The people who came to the north-east of Ireland from Scotland were

Calvinist Presbyterians. The natives were Catholics. These are not any two different religions; they are essentially antithetical. The Reformation was anti-Catholic and the Counter-Reformation was anti-Protestant. The settlers and natives encountered each other at a time when people took religion seriously and when support for competing religions provided an obstacle to inter-marriage and integration.

Religious affiliation is not just a convenient identifying mark, simply signifying team membership: the red bands and green bands of school football teams. Religious ideas and images influence the ways people think and feel; they can structure relationships between groups. Religions readily become involved in social conflict because they help people make sense of their circumstances and they help to justify them.[23] The monotheistic religious traditions of the West offer radical divisions between the good and the bad, the saved and the unsaved, the godly and the ungodly. They also view time, not as the ever-turning wheel of Hinduism or Buddhism, but as a history with a start (the Creation) and an end (the Day of Judgement) and a narrative thrust that elevates certain peoples into heroic destiny-carrying roles and relegates others to the roles of obstacles to be overcome by the Children of Israel. Christianity all too easily becomes, not just a convenient distinguishing mark for an ethnic group, but a central part of its identity. Conflict, especially with an ethnic group identified by a competing religion, strengthens the religious commitment of all participants. One can see this clearly in many of the ethnic disputes that have been released by the collapse of the Soviet Union and its satellites. When Yugoslavia was a stable centralized state controlled by the Communist party, levels of religious attachment were low. With the onset of a series of ethnic wars, the *Catholic* Croatians, *Orthodox* Serbs, and (to a lesser extent) *Muslim* Bosnians have increasingly drawn on their religious identities to deepen what unites them and distance themselves from those they are fighting.

Looking to the thing they had in common which distinguished them from the people among whom they were settling, the Protestant settlers in Ireland were able to explain and justify their privileges by seeing these as the natural result of their having the true religion. If they prospered, it was because it pleased God to let them prosper. If Catholics were poor, it was because they had not been saved and were kept in bondage by their priests. Religion also provided consolation for the subordinate population, and, in the absence of social or political institutions which were free from British influence, the Catholic Church became the main repository of Irish identity.[24]

It is a common feature of many modern societies that industrialization and urbanization have been accompanied by a decline in the influence and importance of religion.[25] Only if particular circumstances give religion an important role other than that of mediating man and God does it retain a high place in the attention of modern peoples and in their politics. That, from the point of settlement, the social groups in competition in Ireland were divided by religion meant that religion remained important. Nothing that has happened since settlement, since the rise of the home-rule movement, or since partition, has reduced the salience of religion. Far from it. De Valera saw the Catholic faith as a crucial element in the rural, Irish-speaking Eire that was his dream and he enshrined that view in the Republic's constitution. Once the South was established as a Catholic country, Protestants were bound to find the idea of a united Ireland abhorrent. Dispassionate observers might argue that the Protestants would be such a large block in any united Ireland that their religious identity could not be threatened by severing the link with Great Britain. Protestants do not see it like that. Instead they point to the virtual disappearance of the Protestants in the South. At partition they were about 11 per cent of the population; now they are under 4 per cent. More recently, Protestants have been able to point to the ability of the Catholic Church to resist attempts to liberalize the Republic's laws on divorce, contraception, and abortion. Ulster Protestants may be little more enthusiastic about these things than Irish Catholics, but still they resent the Catholic Church's power to impose its theology on the laws of the state.

One common weakness of human thought is the desire for simplicity. Another is to suppose that people whose actions we disapprove of must be driven by motives baser than the ones they claim. The two weaknesses combine in Marxist explanations of loyalism and unionism. With the penetrating insight of the ideologue, the Marxist knows that, whatever they say to the contrary, unionists are motivated primarily by a desire to maintain their material advantages over Catholics. Any talk of cultural differences, especially of religious differences, is mere window-dressing, the spurious assertion of a more honourable set of interests than the ones that really drive the action. I have never found the division of interests into material and ideological—with the former being what really gets people out of bed and the latter being 'peripheral', 'secondary', or 'epiphenomenal'—terribly convincing. In the life of any ethnic group, culture and material interests are fused. Protestants undoubtedly enjoyed some material advantages over Catholics (though these have been much exaggerated in subsequent myth-making[26]). Depending on the matter in hand, they might be unconscious of that fact or fully aware of it and ready to explain it as a consequence of their having the right religion and the beneficial social culture that developed from that religion. More importantly for most of them, Protestants enjoyed the privilege of having their symbols and culture accorded pride of place in the affairs of the state. The superiority of their ethnic group was evidenced by the status of their culture.

Why evangelicalism remains an important part of the Protestant ethnic identity can be further appreciated if we note the relative weakness of alternative lines of division. There is nothing at all inevitable about people seeing themselves as part of an ethnic group. Usually we have available to us a variety of groups and matching identities. John can be a member of the Smith family, 'belong to Glasgow', be an Orangeman, work for the Milanda bakery, play in the junior football league, support Rangers, be a trade unionist and a member of the Labour Party, be an elder in the Church of Scotland, and be Scottish. The extent to which Mr Smith invests his sense of self-worth in any of these and other alternatives depends in part on Mr Smith and in part on the circumstances in which he makes his choice. Being a blue-nosed Rangers fan may become so important to Mr Smith that he neglects his wife and loses his family. Or he may stop going to the matches and spend Saturday afternoons with his children. Many people in western Europe live in circumstances where ethnicity and nationalism (which is usually just ethnicity with a specific desire to acquire a sovereign territory for the ethnic group) are not terribly salient. Although racists have tried to stimulate a pressing sense of being English by claiming that it is threatened, for most English people their ethnicity is not something of which they are often aware. It is certainly not something they feel mobilized to defend.

Ireland offers very different circumstances. Here the long history of enduring competition and conflict ensures that ethnic identity is to the forefront of the consciousness of most people. Things happen to people because of their ethnicity and reinforce that sense of belonging to one side rather than another. As Jennifer Todd has neatly described in her distinction between Ulster loyalists and Ulster British, there are for unionists different ways in which they can see themselves, but, and this is my main point, it is always attractive to attend to religious differences because religion most effectively unites large numbers of Protestants and separates them from Catholics. Evangelicalism provides a common bond that crosses divisions of class, region, and denomination and has the added advantage that it provides the clearest rejection of Roman Catholicism. At times when the status of Northern Ireland has not been threatened, it has been possible for simple Britishness to prevail over Ulster loyalism, and it has been possible to seek other identities (through socialism, for example, or ecumenism in religion) which unite people across the confessional division. But once the status of Northern Ireland is challenged, then the question of ethnicity returns in a stark manner: which side are you on? Try it in the form of question and answer. Why be a unionist? To avoid being part of a united Ireland. What is wrong with a united Ireland? It would be a Catholic country. If you do not want to be a Catholic, what are you? A Protestant. If we understand that sequence, we can understand the political success of Ian Paisley and the role of evangelicalism in the thinking of Ulster Protestants.

The connections between religion and politics are not easy to untangle and they certainly cannot be meaningfully reduced to a simple link between individual piety and conservative unionism. To note that evangelical Protestants are likely to support Paisley does not exhaust the influence of religion. I want to suggest that evangelicalism, by virtue of its place in the history of the Protestant people and the logic of the Irish conflict, has become the core of ethnic identity, the guarantor of the ethnic group, and that, from that position, it impinges strongly, albeit subtly, on the responses of large numbers of apparently secular Protestants.

I will say more about this in the final chapter, but a curious feature of much Irish nationalist and left-wing thinking about Ireland is that it takes it for granted that one form of ethnicity and nationalism—Irishness—is natural and inevitable but makes the competing form of Protestant unionism accidental and temporary. The 'Irish people' is seen as a natural formation which needs no explanation and which automatically has characteristics such as a 'right to self-determination'. To strengthen that case and make Ulster Protestants disappear from the equation, the competing Protestant ethnicity is described as merely a product of British imperial manipulation. A more plausible account would be that all ethnic collectivities and all nations are social products brought into being by the complex interaction of cultural and material interests and circumstances. Nations do not create nationalists; nationalists invent nations.[27] For many Protestants in Northern Ireland, Ulster loyalism has displaced the Ulster Britishness which was common prior to the present conflict. As the British government has distanced itself, so Ulster Protestants have had to contemplate the possibility of a future on their own, and the result of that contemplation has not been the one desired by Irish nationalists: recognizing that they are really Irish. Instead Protestants have come increasingly to see themselves as 'Ulster' people. Though independence remains the preferred option of only a very small minority, it is the second best of almost every unionist.[28]

To summarize this section, I am arguing that the Northern Ireland conflict is an ethnic conflict and that religion plays an important part in the identity of the Protestant people. It is for that reason that Ian Paisley has risen to political prominence and that the evangelicalism which he represents has retained symbolic importance for very many Ulster Protestants who are not themselves born-again Christians.

THE GUNMEN AND THE EVANGELICALS

Having described the recent history of the loyalist paramilitaries and the religious and political movements led by Ian Paisley, I now want briefly to look at the relationships between these two worlds. The enduring desire for a simple explanation of everything leads many people to search for common threads in the varied material of life and to suppose that apparently diverse foes are really in cahoots. There are certainly connections between paramilitaries and evangelicals. They inhabit the same country. If they join fraternal organizations, it will be the same ones: the Orange Order, the Apprentice Boys of Derry, and the Royal Black Preceptory. However there is already a difference here. While the men who first led the UVF and UDA were likely to have also been active in such organizations (indeed, the local lodges were often the place to recruit), most terrorists, certainly the later generations, disdained such dull and usually respectable bodies. But the evangelicals were and still are organization men, though in some areas they will be found in the Independent Orange Order rather than the main body. Much the same could be said for political parties. The early paramilitary leaders were often active in the UUP. Since then, they have been more likely to be politically active in their own political organizations (which will be discussed in Chapter 4), and the majority of Protestant terrorists will not have any sort of formal political involvement. The evangelicals, again because they are more likely to be from a social class whose members join and organize things, are much more likely to be politically active and in the DUP. But all of this is only to say that the paramilitary and evangelical worlds are both subsections of loyalism. The same thing could be said of republican terrorists, constitutional nationalists, and the Catholic Church. They are all part of the same world.

There are also connections of common purpose. There are

many differences of image and emphasis, of course, but the paramilitaries and the evangelicals share common goals: keeping Northern Ireland British and, if that fails, keeping Northern Ireland out of the Irish Republic.

But when people talk of links between the paramilitaries and the Paisleyites, they are looking for something both narrower and more sensational. To put it bluntly, they want to find Paisley holding a gun. There are some tenuous links. In the 1950s Paisley was active in a pressure group called Ulster Protestant Action, as was William Nixon, an ex-police inspector and later independent unionist MP at Stormont. It is claimed that Nixon led sectarian murder gangs in Belfast in the early 1920s, but, as he was never charged with any offence, let alone convicted, and won a libel case against an author who accused him of such activities, it is difficult to assume that a young man who thirty years later was impressed by Nixon's resolute unionism was consciously flirting with a sectarian killer.[29] Less tenuous is the connection between Spence's UVF and Paisley's UPV: as we have seen, some people were active in both organizations. But again, even his most hostile critics do not demonstrate that Paisley either knew of or condoned such ties.[30]

Where the link is strongest is in Paisley's periodic attempts to set up his own paramilitary forces. A number of times during the Troubles Paisley has argued that the security situation is so threatening to Protestants that there is a need for a 'third force' of vigilantes to complement the army and the police. It has to be said, however, that most of these initiatives have got no further than speechifying or holding meetings at which men could sign up to show their willingness to defend Ulster if the need arose. On only two occasions did a militia take even the loosest shape. In 1981, in a protest against discussions between Margaret Thatcher and Charles Haughey, the British and Irish prime ministers, Paisley organized a parade of 500 men on a wet hillside in Country Antrim. For an invited audience of journalists, on a command, the men took out and waved their firearms certificates! In November of the year that saw tensions considerably heightened by the republican hunger-strikes and the murder of Robert Bradford MP, Paisley led a march of 15,000 men through the County Down town of Newtownards. Groups of this 'Third Force' in Tyrone and Fermanagh mounted a few night-time roadblocks as a publicity exercise but did not engage in seriously illegal paramilitary activities and the movement soon petered out.

Five years later there was a more serious paramilitary initiative in the form of Ulster Resistance. Unlike the Third Force, this was not Paisley's idea. By and large the paramilitaries have recruited from the urban areas of Belfast and its satellite estates, and, to a much lesser extent, other large towns. In contrast to the 1912 UVF, the present UDA and UVF have not been popular with rural Protestants. In the aftermath of the Anglo-Irish accord, a number of rural evangelicals from County Armagh proposed forming a new paramilitary force. Paisley and his deputy Peter Robinson agreed to give political leadership to the group and delivered the usual rousing martial speeches at a recruiting rally in Belfast's Ulster Hall. Paisley said: 'There are many like myself who would like to see the agreement brought down by democratic means, but wouldn't we all be fools if we weren't prepared.'[31] Ulster Resistance claimed to be vetting, training, and drilling recruits, but like previous initiatives it fizzled out. When, in November 1988, Ulster Resistance berets were discovered in a County Armagh arms dump containing parts of stolen Shorts missiles, Paisley and Robinson issued a statement summarizing their initial involvement and adding: 'Some time later we were informed that the organization had been put on ice and our association and contact ended. At no time during our association was anything done which was outside the law and no member of the movement was ever charged with an offence.'[32]

The paramilitary view of Paisley is extremely hostile. One operator described his groups as a 'turd force'. Most were extremely rude about Paisley's bluster. To the hard men, Paisley is an opportunist and a coward who makes encouragingly militant noises but then condemns the gunmen when they turn his rhetoric into action. Liberal and nationalist critics of Paisley are fond of reviving the tale of Hugh McClean. McClean was one of Spence's UVF men. In the prosecution case at his trial for the murder of barman Peter Ward, the police read a statement (which

McClean denied making) in which he is supposed to have said: 'I am terribly sorry I ever heard of that man Paisley or decided to follow him. I am definitely ashamed of myself to be in such a position.'[33] Given what we now know about police 'verbals', it is worth considering how little that statement approximates to working-class Belfast speech patterns and how well it suited the RUC at the time to blacken Paisley's reputation. The important point is that, if McClean genuinely held those sentiments, he was unique among UVF men. For the terrorists, if Paisley had a fault, it was not that he persuaded them to acts they later regretted but that he sought to maintain a line between legitimate unionist protest and their 'vile sectarian murders'. To the loyalist terrorists, Paisley was and still is the Grand Old Duke of York, and every march up the hill is followed by the retreat down again.

Most Paisleyites are equally unimpressed by the gunmen. We should understand the general theory of violence held by most evangelicals. Like the original Covenanters (and most modern political theorists), they believe that the citizen has an obligation to support the state and to resign to the state the right to use violence. Only if the state reneges on its obligations (by patently failing to provide protection to its citizens or by expelling people from citizenship) are private individuals entitled to take up arms and practise violence. Most evangelicals (and thus far that includes Paisley) do not believe that such a point has yet been reached. Preparations for self-defence that stop short of breaking the law are fine, but vigilante violence is unacceptable. Hence Paisley and other leading evangelicals regularly criticize the murders of the UDA and UVF.

There is another set of reasons why most evangelicals are unhappy with the terrorists and that is that most are not saved and lack the appropriate civic virtues. As would be the case on the republican side, many Protestant terrorists are close enough to the tradition of their religion to send their wives and children to Sunday school and church and may even talk with pride about how God-fearing are their wives, but they are not Bible-believing born-again Christians. They smoke and drink and swear, and some take drugs and sell pornography and engage in loose sexual behaviour. Northern Ireland is sufficiently polarized for the logic of 'my enemy's enemy is my friend' to cause evangelicals to be more understanding of loyalist violence than their principles should allow them to be, but there is still a vast gulf between the two worlds.

As an aside and for the sake of completeness, it is worth adding that not all evangelicals would have the political involvement of the Paisleyites or those in the main churches who share many of their views. There is in Ulster a *pietistic* evangelical tradition which sees religion as an alternative to the ways of the world and which stresses the importance of avoiding worldly contamination. Especially strong in working-class urban areas, a gospel-hall and Pentecostal tradition serves as a way out of the everyday world and offers an alternative persona and career for many former terrorists. This world's view of politics was neatly shown in a running battle of posters. In 1986 unionist-controlled councils signalled their attitude to the Anglo-Irish accord by displaying large banners which read 'Ulster Says No'. Pastor James McConnell's Metropolitan Church of God in north Belfast put up a similar-sized banner which used the same design style to say: 'Ulster Needs Christ'. When, two years later, the councils replaced the first banners with ones reading 'Ulster Still Says No', McConnell changed his to read 'Ulster Still Needs Christ'! It is worth adding that there is even a sizeable proportion of Paisley's Free Presbyterian Church that believes that its close association with a particular political position is compromising its primary goal of winning souls for Christ.

It is my clear impression that, though the paramilitaries (usually urban, secular, and working class) and the evangelicals (often rural and certainly religious) are occasionally forced into working side-by-side (as in the 1974 UWC strike), there is little love lost between them. They inhabit different worlds with very different values and culture and only *in extremis* can they set aside their mutual loathing. None the less there is an important truth buried in the cheap accusation that Paisley and his people (even if inadvertently) encourage violence: they are not pacifists. The rural evangelicals of the Free Presbyterian and Irish Presbyterian churches are perfectly happy with the idea that there is some point at which the failure of the state to defend them releases them from their obligation to be law-abiding. In 1912 such people were the backbone of the UVF, and we can imagine circumstances in which they would again take up arms.

2. THE DISMAL VISION

THE dual purpose of this book is to assess loyalists' thinking about their position and to offer a corrective to much of our thinking about loyalists. To lay the foundations for what follows in this chapter, I want to begin by establishing what the rest of the chapter then attempts to explain: the extent of loyalist unhappiness with the recent past and the present. To do this I will draw attention to what seem the most significant facts from the loyalist world of 1993: the high level of loyalist paramilitary violence and the strength of the DUP vote.

Despite the lesson of the 1974 UWC strike, most liberal observers of Northern Ireland and certainly most government advisers still see the best way forward as being the cultivation of a liberal 'centre' made up of constitutional nationalists represented by the SDLP and liberal unionists represented by whoever in the UUP can be persuaded to play the role left vacant by the departure from politics of Brian Faulkner. Or, to describe the same policy facing outwards, the aim is to promote social, economic, and political policies that reduce support for republicanism on the nationalist side and for the loyalist paramilitaries and the DUP on the unionist side.

Northern Ireland in the 1990s offers little to encourage such hopes. The IRA continues to go about its business, and the UDA and UVF have returned to their assassination campaigns. The extent to which the loyalists had moderated can be seen in the death tolls (see the Appendix). The dip came in 1978, when loyalists killed only eight people compared to twenty-five in the year before and 113 in 1976. In the eight years from 1978 to 1985 loyalists were responsible for an average of 8.5 murders per year. In the aftermath of the Anglo-Irish accord, the average went up to

18.6 per year for the years 1986–90. Then it rocketed. The totals fell a long way short of the roughly 100 victims per year of 1972–6, but at forty for 1991 and thirty-two for 1992 they still represented what Northern Ireland felt to be a major shock wave. Far from producing the much advertised decline in violence, the Anglo-Irish accord and the Stevens inquiry were followed by a considerable increase in loyalist paramilitary activity, primarily from the UDA/UFF but with the UVF also stepping up its killing.

The other major sign that loyalists were not moderating their opposition to government policy came with the 1993 elections. As already noted, the DUP does badly in comparison with the UUP when it is in coalition with the older and larger party (and hence is prevented from criticizing liberal tendencies in that party) and when there are no electoral contests at a level between local government elections and Westminster elections. Hence the late 1980s had shown a decline in the DUP's fortunes and it was widely hoped that the decline would continue. In advance of the May 1993 local government elections, the *Irish News* gave one article the headline: 'Roasting for Paisley in polls is UUP plan'. It might have added that this was also the plan of Her Majesty's Government. Instead of being roasted, the DUP did rather well, as did Sinn Fein in its contest for Catholic votes. Boundary changes meant that there were in 1993 sixteen more seats available than previously. The middle-of-the-road Alliance Party increased from thirty-nine to forty-four. The UUP gained four seats, from 193 to 197. And the SDLP also gained four seats, from 121 to 127. Sinn Fein went up from forty-three to fifty-one seats. The DUP actually ended up with slightly fewer seats— down from 110 to 103—but, in the context of the decline in DUP support in previous polls, and the decline in its vote at the Westminster general election in 1991, this stability was widely seen as a considerable victory for the DUP, and the party is now looking forward to Ian Paisley retaining or even improving on his massive personal vote in the 1994 European elections.

As a further piece of scene-setting I would like to mention the results of a poll which, though they cannot be generalized far, are still worth considering. The *Ulster News Letter* invited readers to phone in and say whether they supported loyalist violence, thought it could in any circumstances be justified, and whether they thought loyalist gunmen would stop if the IRA ended its campaign. Out of 4,000 calls received, 42 per cent of callers said they supported loyalist violence, almost half said that they felt it was justified in some circumstances, and what the *Irish News* called a 'resounding' 82 per cent thought loyalists would stop killing if the IRA did.[1] Given that the respondents selected themselves rather than being selected to be representative of the unionist population, it is important not to make too much of these data, but they could be read as evidence that the unionist majority in Northern Ireland was deeply unhappy. I will now turn to the reasons for what unionists, belatedly borrowing a phrase from nationalists, described as their increasing alienation.

If we are to understand the loyalist and the broader unionist view of the world, we need to see the lie of the land through those lenses; an exercise in comprehension, not in criticism or endorsement. I will try to describe and fill in those observations that have been most frequently made when I have asked my interviewees to tell me what are the most striking features of the changes in Northern Ireland both since the start of the Troubles and in the period from 1989 to 1993.

VIOLENCE AND LOSS

'Ulster used to be a great wee place. Really lovely and always very quiet'; so spoke an elderly Protestant lady from Bangor, County Down. Her husband and she had holidayed in the province in the 1940s and decided to settle because it was such an attractive peaceful place. Those who had lived through the turmoil of the 1920s might have described Northern Ireland differently, but her nostalgia is a central part of most loyalist thinking.

The first and most obvious feature of the recent history of Ulster unionists is displacement. At the start of this century, with a Liberal government intent on giving independence to Ireland, the unionist position looked extremely precarious. However, the formation of the 1912 UVF, its glorious performance in the First

World War, and the creation of the Stormont mini-state with its assured unionist majority, turned disaster into victory and created, for a short period, a unionist golden age. It was not perfect. Many unionists felt aggrieved that, with 25 per cent of the votes cast in all Ireland elections in 1918, they got only 18 per cent of the island, but what they had seemed secure. They could be annoyed that the government of the Free State had reneged on its 1925 treaty obligations to develop 'friendly relations' and 'neighbourly comradeship'[2] and that de Valera's constitution for the Irish Republic laid claim to Northern Ireland, but they had peace and stability and Ulster was a 'great wee place'.

Since then, with a turning-point that is put variously between the appointment of Terence O'Neill as Prime Minister in 1963 and 1972 when the British government closed down the Stormont parliament and assumed direct control of the province, there has been a steady decline. The civil-rights movement, which very quickly turned into old-fashioned nationalism, destabilized Northern Ireland and set in motion a series of changes, very few of which can be seen by unionists as an improvement. Some—the disbanding of the B Special Constabulary, for example—weakened the ability of unionists to defend the political status quo or themselves. Others—the 1974 Sunning-dale agreement with its power-sharing Executive and Council of Ireland, for example—are seen as the British government deliberately undermining the status of Northern Ireland as part of the United Kingdom. Though at any time since 1969 an optimistic unionist could take heart that things were not worse, it is hard to see the recent past as anything other than a decline from security to precariousness, from domination to impotence, from potentate to pariah, and from heroic defenders of the British Empire to an international embarrassment.

It may well be that the IRA will never win in the sense of creating an Ireland in its preferred image, but, in comparison with those of the 1920s and the 1950s, the present IRA campaign is a considerable success. After twenty-five years it is still going strong. Although the security forces succeed in pre-empting bombings or ambushing active service units, the IRA can apparently still murder at will and can bomb the heart out of

Protestant towns. From 1969, supported by liberal unionists, constitutional nationalists, and the Dublin government, the British government has presented every reform with the argument that accommodating the legitimate demands of nationalists will isolate republican terrorists and reduce the IRA's capability. And yet, despite all the political and social changes, the IRA seems as capable as ever.

On 8 November 1987, as people gathered for the Remembrance Day ceremony at the Cenotaph in Enniskillen, Fermanagh, an IRA bomb exploded, killing eleven and very seriously injuring a further nineteen. Of all the bombings that could have been recalled, this one stayed with so many of those I interviewed because of the symbolism of the targeting. Although many Irish Catholics have served in the British forces, the Northern Ireland conflict has so polarized reactions to the Crown that in Ulster publicly commemorating the dead of two world wars, no matter that the conduct and eventual victories of the Western allies in those wars is almost universally approved of, is something rarely done by Catholics. Hence the bombers could be fairly sure that their victims would be Protestants—not people actively 'oppressing' the minority, not representatives of the state, but ordinary Fermanagh Protestants engaged in a solemn act of remembrance for the dead of just wars. As one elderly farmer bitterly put it: 'And there's people blind enough to say the IRA is not sectarian. Be sure their sins will find them out!'

More recently a series of large bombs has torn the hearts out of Protestant towns and housing estates. What is often described as an attack on 'economic targets' has become very clearly a sectarian policy of attacking Protestant economic targets. In May 1991 a 300-lb. bomb exploded in a Protestant housing estate in Cookstown, damaging 120 houses (twenty-six had to be demolished) and making hundreds of people homeless. In March 1992 Lurgan was the target. In November 1992 a massive bomb wrecked the centre of Bangor, an overwhelmingly Protestant town in a local council district that is more than 90 per cent Protestant. The same month another largely Protestant town, Coleraine, was also blown up with a 500-lb. bomb in a van. In May it was the turn of Portadown and Magherafelt with damage estimated at £8m. and £5m. respectively. Central Belfast was bombed twice in July, the same month that the centre was blown out of Newtownards, and again in August. And those were the ones that went off. In 1993 three enormous bombs (between 2,000 and 3,000 lb. of explosives) were found in County Armagh, a 600-lb. bomb was defused in Cookstown, and the Gardai found three 1,500-lb. bombs in County Donegal. As one elderly evangelical said: 'There just seems no end to it.'

The sense of shock at the ease with which the IRA could attack Protestant areas was nicely expressed by the Moderator of the Presbyterian Church, who said in Newtownards: 'I am very sad to see this. I come from Dungannon, a place where we have become used to bomb attacks but somehow I never thought I would see such scenes in North Down.'[3] Although, as a politician, he was speaking in part for effect, we can take as sincere Unionist MP John Taylor's view that, though he never thought he would have to say it, he now felt that the IRA was indeed winning.[4] Something similar was said by all the evangelicals I interviewed. Presumably because they like to think that their terror is having an effect, loyalist paramilitaries were less pessimistic about the IRA campaign, but most were also scathing about the government's ability to stop republican violence.

Without any prompting, many respondents talked about the significance of IRA terror for their understanding of community relations. They made the point that there is little sign that the IRA's campaign is making it unpopular with Catholics.

Twenty years now people has been telling us that ordinary Catholics is not gunmen, that they is like us. Every time there is some murder down here, the priest says this is the work of outsiders and that there is never any trouble down here and everything is luvvy-duvvy. Well I ask you, who was it that voted for Bobby Sands MP IRA Man? Thirty and a half thousand of ordinary decent Catholics in this constituency [Fermanagh and South Tyrone] who are not gunmen voted for a gunman. And who still votes for Sinn Fein? I am not a bitter man and I have raised five children not to be bitter and I can tell you that the ordinary Catholic does not mind benefiting from the work of the gunman. When the gunman kills a farmer, who buys that farm? When the gunman kills a shopkeeper, who buys that shop? The ordinary Catholic tolerates the

IRA and votes for the IRA and takes the benefits from the IRA because they want us out of our country.

So spoke a middle-aged Tyrone farmer. A coal merchant from a small village in North Antrim expressed very similar sentiments:

You have to know people here a very long time before they will talk to you but I will tell you this. When those students started the trouble in 19 and 69, I said to myself: 'That's just rabble rousers. Ordinary Catholics up around this way are a decent sort.' But as every year goes in I have more trouble believing that. They have had long enough to stop the IRA. Everyone says they are not supporting the IRA but then who is? You are an educated man. You tell me. Who is?

For those who live in Northern Ireland there is an awesome unreality about the response of outsiders who greet every new atrocity by announcing that this time the IRA has gone too far. This time they have revolted their own supporters. For anyone with a memory, such trite searching for silver linings is an insult. Consider the record of peace campaigns. In August 1976 three young children from the same family, one a 6-month-old boy in a pram, were killed when a gunman's getaway car went out of control. Two days later 1,000 women demonstrated in Andersonstown. Two days after that, the crowd was 10,000. The popular despair was mobilized into the Peace People movement. There were mass rallies. The founders were awarded the Nobel Peace Prize. There was no peace. A decade further on and we saw the wave of sympathy generated by the forgiving response of Enniskillen man Gordon Wilson to the death of his daughter in the Remembrance Day bombing. Conor Cruise O'Brien, not normally one to fall prey to easy optimism, said: 'Will Enniskillen prove a turning point? There is some reason to hope that it may. Certainly, I cannot remember a time when the ambivalence count has been so low . . . It is as if that single spectacular explosion so lit up the landscape that people suddenly became aware of what the IRA is about and what helping it means.'[5] Two academic writers on terrorism described Enniskillen as a 'propaganda setback for the IRA'.[6] The same hopes were expressed after the Warrington bombing in March 1993 killed two young children. Each of these murders and many more have had no discernible long-term impact on IRA support in Northern Ireland. Indeed, the Warrington bombing showed clearly that many people were not easily shifted from their political positions by the IRA's actions. There was a strong and spontaneous emotional response in Dublin, but this was followed by equally popular counter-demonstrations of support for the nationalist dead in the North. Most significantly, the Sinn Fein vote at the local government elections shortly after the Warrington bomb showed IRA support holding up, not declining. The party may have lost what little electoral support it had in the South and in 1993 it had to accept the indignity of Dublin City Council banning its annual conference from the Mansion House. But it still attracts more than 10 per cent of the voters in the North.

There is a core of people whose hatred for the other side is so great that any hurt inflicted on them, no matter how awful, is a cause for rejoicing. They use wall graffiti to present numbers of fatalities as the scores of football matches: 'RUC 0—IRA 2'. They act out depraved jokes. After the death of IRA hunger-striker Bobby Sands, I saw a skeleton hanging in the back of a loyalist bus with 'Diet the Bobby Sands way' written underneath it. When the notorious 'Shankill Butchers' gang was convicted for a long series of horrendous murders of randomly selected Catholics, some loyalist football fans chanted 'Shankill Butchers' in approval. On an Orange Lodge parade past the betting shop on the lower Ormeau Road where five men had recently been murdered by the UFF, some marchers held up five fingers to taunt those residents who shouted abuse at the Orangemen. The same thing happened at the funeral procession for Thomas Begley, the young IRA man who blew himself up with the Shankill Road fish shop. Some republican mourners taunted Protestant onlookers by holding up nine fingers to signify Begley's nine Protestant victims.[7] A Sinn Fein official told a journalist of waking to see 'Shankill fish—nine for a pound' painted on a wall in his street.[8] An inquest of a soldier murdered by the IRA was told of women laughing at the fatally injured young man as he lay dying in an Armagh street.[9] I suspect that such callousness is considerably more common than might be inferred from the sanitized justifications of the killers and from the *pro-forma* response of their critics (where words such as 'evil' are used so readily that they cease to invoke any response other than the yawning thought that they would say that). However, I also suspect that most people's response to violence is profoundly ambivalent—a mixture of outrage and sympathy in which the hesitation of the 'but' plays a large part: 'We are totally opposed to murder *but*, so long as they kill us, it is understandable that young men on our side will retaliate.'

Two principles seem to govern attitudes to murder. Most people have some notion of deserved and undeserved death, of the legitimate targets and the innocent victims. For example, had it succeeded, it is hard to imagine many Protestants regretting the UDA's attempt in March 1984 to murder Gerry Adams. On the other hand, it is hard to imagine many Protestants approving of the death of a woman and her son killed when young loyalists torched their house (their sin was to be a mixed religion family living in a loyalist area). To be killed is a terrible thing, but some people deserve it and others do not.

Competing with that attempt to preserve some sort of morality and ethical judgement about the fate of *individuals* is the pressure that the conflict itself generates to see everything in *group* or ethnic terms. At the very start of the Troubles loyalist journals such as the *Loyalist News* used the following argument to justify the murder of Catholics (in this particular instance, the bombing of McGurk's Bar, which killed fifteen people including two children). The victims were IRA men. Some of them were IRA men. If they were not active members, then they were supporters of the IRA. If they were not supporters of the IRA, then at the very least they had silently acquiesced in IRA atrocities in that they did nothing to root the IRA out of their areas. And, even if they were not guilty of that crime, they were nationalists who were willing to benefit politically from the actions of the IRA and were thus almost as responsible as the IRA. Therefore, all Catholics are equally responsible for IRA violence. The distinction between 'guilty' and 'innocent' Catholics dissolved.[10]

Judging people as individuals is the logic of the liberal democracy; judging people by their ethnicity and imputing to all the character of some is the logic of tribal or ethnic or national war. Beyond my own impressions based on reading loyalist and unionist publications, reading books, listening to sermons, or talking to people, there is no evidence that I can offer to support this conclusion, but I am convinced that the course of the Ulster conflict has been accompanied by a steady increase in the amount of ethnic judgement. The political reforms were intended to win the allegiance of the Catholic minority and thus remove support for the IRA. Unionists have been forced to give up a great deal and they have not got what was implicitly promised. The loss of political power and of a sense of superiority might have been bearable had they been accompanied by peace, but the Catholic minority does not deliver peace. One conclusion loyalists draw is that all those protestations about the difference between republican gunmen and ordinary decent Catholics were hollow. The persistence of republican violence after the legitimate grievances of the minority have been addressed and redressed proves that this conflict is not about civil rights; it is about ethnic power.

In many of my conversations, talk about violence led to criticism of the British government's security policy. Against the view frequently attributed to security-force experts that the IRA can never be totally defeated militarily, there is widespread suspicion in loyalist and wider unionist circles that the government is not trying to win. At a meeting in Derry in November 1993 held to discuss 'Protestant alienation', the most warmly received contribution came from a Scot who had served in the army in Belfast in the early 1970s and whose son was now serving in Northern Ireland. His insistence that he had had to work with one hand tied behind his back and that now his son was in the same position was loudly cheered. Different people and different groups have their own preferred 'magic ingredient'. The DUP is keen on the death penalty and a 'steel ring' of road blocks around republican areas. The UUP security spokesman wants internment. Others feel that the balance of judicial rights has been tilted too far in favour of the terrorists. Many of those I talked to had no single innovation in mind but merely wanted the government to try harder. The inability of the security forces to prevent IRA atrocities was compared unfavourably with the

success of the Stormont government in 1920 and the 1950s—
'The B men would soon have sorted that lot out!'—and the
continuing violence was interpreted in the light of the general
perception of decay and decline and betrayal.

ETHNIC-CLEANSING

If the fact of IRA violence was uppermost in the minds of most
loyalists, the *purpose* of it was close behind. The IRA has always
insisted that it does not condone sectarian violence.[11] From the
very start there were those, usually the people at the sharp end of
the border campaign, who believed that the IRA was engaged in a
very deliberate campaign to force Protestants out of the border
areas and thus gradually move more of Ulster into the Irish
Republic. That they were most obviously vulnerable led many
Protestant men in the border counties of Armagh, Fermanagh,
Derry, and Tyrone to join first the B Specials and then the RUC
Reserve or the Ulster Defence Regiment as part-time policemen
or soldiers. This meant that the IRA could justify murdering them
on the grounds that they were members of the security forces, or
had been members of the security forces, or were related to
members of the security forces. To use the term made popular
during the Bosnian war of 1992–3, the targeted population saw
this simply as 'ethnic-cleansing'. In the twenty years since the
early 1970s, that analysis has moved from being the paranoia of
the few to being the consensus view of the majority. Now a
middle-of-the-road Presbyterian minister uses the phrase to
describe what the IRA has done to the Protestants of his small
village of Pomeroy. Buried in his graveyard are six victims of
republicanism. Dr John Dunlop, the mild-mannered Moderator of
the Presbyterian Church in Ireland, added his voice to that of
Revd Bingham, and the Church of Ireland Primate Archbishop
Robin Eames agreed that the IRA was intent on driving
Protestants out of the border areas.[12]

Father Denis Faul, a priest who has done his best to persuade
Catholics from supporting the IRA, completely missed the point
when he responded to claims of ethnic-cleansing by saying that

local Catholics could remember no instance of a Protestant family being driven out of its home or farm by threats, intimidation, or force in the last fifty years.[13] Killing the male head of a household or murdering the eldest son of elderly farming parents seems a pretty effective way of persuading people to leave an area.

Put simply, though the IRA may see its terror as being directed against individuals who in their view deserve it and against the institutions of the state, Protestants see it as a murderous attack on Protestants, and even Catholic leaders are coming to see it like that. Cardinal Cahal Daly in April 1993 used a lecture at the Queen's University of Belfast to say: 'I want to voice my condemnation of murders of Protestant farmers and workers, which have been a feature of the IRA campaign since it began. This campaign cannot but be seen by Protestants as a concerted campaign on this whole community, intended to drive them from their homes, particularly in exposed areas.'[14]

POPULATION CHANGES

The unionism that developed in opposition to the Irish home-rule movement in the late nineteenth century wanted to keep the whole island of Ireland within the United Kingdom. It was only when it became clear that the main game was lost that unionists became 'Ulster' unionists and argued for the retention of the six northern counties—which could be described as the largest area which would still ensure a clear Protestant majority or as what was rightly their share, depending on your preference. From 1921 to 1971 the population balance remained much the same, the higher Catholic fertility being compensated for by higher Catholic rates of migration. When the Papal encyclical *Humanae vitae* strenuously reaffirmed the Church's opposition to artificial contraception, many evangelical Protestants interpreted it as Rome's strategy to undermine the last stronghold of the evangelical gospel by encouraging Catholics to outbreed the Protestants. This was dismissed by liberal unionists as the paranoia of fundamentalists, but the three census decades from

1961 to 1991 have once again raised the numbers question. In 1961 the census gave the Catholic population as 34.9 per cent; in 1991 it was given as 38.4 per cent. Although the number of those who refused to co-operate was not on the scale of 1981, there were still in 1991 over 7 per cent who refused to state their religion, and this forces us to estimate the actual proportions. Informed reasoning from other sources (such as the Continuous Household Survey) put the total Catholic proportion of the population at around the 40 per cent mark.[15]

Changes in overall population balance are dramatized by movements of population as people respond to the threat of violence by moving to areas which are more solidly 'their' area. Essentially this means Protestants moving east. Old black-and-white movies about the last war often began with the scene-setting device of a map of Europe which gradually changes its shading to represent the German advance. Many Protestants have a similar mental vision of the spread of Catholic preponderance from west to east.

The 1991 census report shows that the Protestant proportion of the population is increasing in only five of twenty-six local district council areas, and those areas are all on the eastern side of the province: Newtownabbey, Carrickfergus, Larne, North Down, and Ards. Eleven of the twenty-six districts now have Catholic majorities, and there are four or five others which are over 44 per cent Catholic and where the Catholic proportion is increasing.

In Derry (which was called Londonderry until the newly established nationalist majority on the council changed the name) the shift in population has been particularly marked, divided as the city is by the River Foyle. Protestants have all but abandoned the west city side of the river and concentrated on the eastern Waterside or moved further afield to Eglinton or Limavady. In August 1993, when only four of their members were left on the city side, the Baptists of Derry opened their new church on the Waterside and closed their old premises in the city centre. As DUP councillor Gregory Campbell explained: 'The closure of the Baptist church, which was fairly small, is in line with what has been happening in the city over the last 23 years. The drift is due to a number of factors. It's obviously related to the security position. Protestants feel safer on the east bank. They feel the west bank is ground which is not well-disposed to them. It's alien territory almost.'[16] According to a Tyrone business man who has been collecting data on population shifts, Coalisland in Tyrone was 20 per cent Protestant in 1965. Now it is 2 per cent. The population has doubled but there are only 120 Protestants left in Coalisland. It used to have a state primary school and a thriving Church of Ireland. The school has now closed and the church is merged with other parishes and only hangs on because people return to worship on Sunday. 'Or you take what has happened to Moy. People think of Moy as a perfect example of a neat well-kept wee Protestant village. It was 60 per cent Protestant. It is now 65 per cent Roman Catholic. Leading Protestant business-men have been murdered out of Moy. My predecessor in the [Orange] Lodge was shot out.' The shifts are also seen starkly in Belfast, where there has been a massive reduction in the Protestant population of west and north Belfast. The Greater Shankill area, once the soul of unionist Ulster, has now only a third of the 80,000 people it had twenty years ago.[17] The decline of the Protestant population of north Belfast can be seen in the schools. In 1971 there were nine state secondary schools. By the mid-1980s there were five and they were short of pupils. Cairnmartin was built for 2,000 children; it now teaches 300. In the Catholic Ardoyne, half the population is under 25; on the other side of the tall 'peace-line' wall, in the Protestant streets of Alliance and Glenbryn, the residents are elderly people and pensioners.[18]

The population changes mean pressure on space and space is land and the land is what the whole conflict is all about, in urban as much as in rural areas. Hence it is no surprise to discover that north Belfast, with its tangled interfaces, has been the site for one in five of the casualties of the conflict.

There has been a reverse in the normal patterns of migration. Instead of working-class Catholics, it is now middle-class Protestants who leave the province. The children of middle-class families used to go to university in Dublin (at Trinity College, which used to be a Protestant establishment) or in

England. But they returned. Now 44 per cent of Protestants who enter higher education (compared with 27 per cent of Catholics) study in Britain and very many do not return.[19] For middle-class Protestants, the absence of their children is a potent sign of their own decline. For rural border Protestants, it is the headstones in graveyards and the farms changing hands. For working-class Protestants, it is the changing religious complexion of streets in north and west Belfast.

The impartial observer might immediately respond that the loyalist obsession with changes in population misses the crucial point that not all Catholics are nationalists. That is indeed true and at one level very important. Though the percentages vary and the polling techniques under-represent the views of working-class republicans, every poll taken has shown a sizeable number of Catholics who wish Northern Ireland to remain within the United Kingdom for the foreseeable future. A MORI poll in 1992 found that number to be more than half.[20] Even when the question put withdrawal ten years away, only one in every three Catholic respondents said he or she was in favour of a united Ireland. Twenty years earlier a 1972 *Belfast Telegraph* poll showed only 39 per cent of Catholics in favour of a united Ireland.[21] A major attitude survey six years later showed 83 per cent of Catholics agreeing that 'a United Ireland is a worthwhile objective provided it can be achieved by peaceful means' but only 39 per cent chose a united Ireland as their preferred policy option.[22] Many Catholics vote for Alliance and some vote unionist. Many who vote for the SDLP do so, not because they wish to see a united Ireland in their lifetimes but to register their unhappiness with parts of the circumstances of Northern Catholics.

This information is known to unionists and is regularly deployed in arguments about the will of the majority, but, as I will argue at a number of points in this book, the psychological impact of that information is overridden by the many facets of the conflict that require attention to the simple ethnic division.

There are differences between loyalists and more moderate unionists in what details they add to their general perception of being squeezed by the Catholic population. Evangelicals see the growth in the Catholic population as a popish plot. There is a secular explanation which attributes Catholic growth to the improvidence of poor Catholics who prefer to breed and collect state subsidies for their offspring rather than limit their family size to what they can afford. More moderate unionists may explain the differences in fertility as an unfortunate by-product of poverty. Whatever explanation is favoured, the general image that now confronts all unionists is one of becoming a minority in what was once their land. And this holds even when unionists are thinking of the competing ethnic group not as a threat to the constitution but as competition for resources within Northern Ireland.

LOCAL COUNCIL POWER

The population shifts are both reflected in, and symbolized by, the changing composition of local authorities. Local government in Northern Ireland is far weaker than its counterpart in most other political systems and in Great Britain. This is partly because its powers were set at a time when the local councils had above them a devolved government at Stormont to manage an area and population that is smaller than that of the Strathclyde Region in Scotland. It is also partly because the British government has tried to solve aspects of the Northern Ireland problem by removing powers from elected representatives who were thought to be using their powers in housing allocation, for example, to benefit their own people.[23] However, councils still have considerable budgets to provide leisure amenities, to support community action groups, and to encourage small-scale economic initiatives, and all of these can be sources of contention. Furthermore, councils both are potent symbols and offer access to potent symbols. Hence they can be used for deliberate affronts to the other side. Unionists used the councils they controlled as part of their 'Ulster Says No' campaign against the 1985 Anglo-Irish accord. Nationalists used their control of the city council to drop the 'London' from the 'Derry' in the name of the council and town.

For unionists the crucial point of the last twenty years has been loss. There was a time when a clear majority of councils were controlled by unionists. And then they started to fall. By the mid-1980s most of the councils west of the Bann had gone, and now even councils to the east have been threatened. Though they have not yet lost their unionist majorities, in 1993 both Lisburn and Carrickfergus councils elected non-unionist Catholic mayors. The exodus of Protestants from Derry was confirmed when for the first time in the city's history no unionist was elected from the Irish Republic side of the River Foyle. Belfast City Council, whose ornate chambers housed the Northern Ireland parliament before the Stormont buildings were completed, has since 1988 become symbolically important as the venue for bitter arguments between unionists and Sinn Fein councillors. It now has a unionist majority of just one seat.

Loyalists believe that nationalist councils discriminate against Protestant areas in the distribution of funds for economic regeneration and community services. Because it is not easy to be certain what proportion of each ethnic group uses certain facilities, it is not possible unambiguously to identify any particular item of public fund spending as being 'for Catholics' or 'for Protestants', but one examination of Derry City Council's 1993/4 allocation of £272,200 for various community projects suggests that only some 5 per cent is being given to organizations working in Protestant areas.[24] It is interesting to note that the SDLP politicians who control Derry council have an entirely different view of their administration. They believe it to be fair. They are impressed by their own tolerance in rotating symbolic offices with unionists. They regard the exodus of Protestants from the city as their choice.

Alienation is a question for the unionist community to address. How can they include themselves? In the tercentenary of the Siege, where we even had a Siege Symphony, unionists boycotted it, even though it celebrated their history. It hurt us deeply last year when there was a campaign to have boundaries redrawn in an attempt to partition Derry. Even in Derry, where we've been so generous, they wanted partition to control their own area.[25]

Here we have the familiar tone of the master hurt by his servant's lack of gratitude—a sentiment heard often between 1922 and 1972 when Protestants expressed incomprehension at the attitude of ingrate Catholics. It says something about the integrity of the conflict that not only is the posture of the under-dog reproduced—Protestants now complain about lack of services and discrimination—but the psychology of the superior has also been preserved: claim to be virtuous and blame the victims.

FAIRNESS AND SECTARIANISM

Unionists do not approve of discrimination. In theory, they are very much in favour of treating all people fairly. After all, that is their legacy. There is a historically sound argument for saying that individualism and egalitarianism are by-products of the Protestant Reformation. Evangelicals would argue that it is because the Protestant faith makes each individual solely responsible for his or her salvation (no one else can intercede for our souls) that the social consequences of Protestantism are superior to those of Catholicism. Protestant apologists frequently contrast the human-rights records of Protestant regimes with those of Catholic countries. Yet there is now considerable loyalist anger about social policy in the province, especially with regard to 'fair-employment' initiatives.

Again the most useful way of thinking about this is in terms of ambivalence. Like the old joke of the neighbour who insists that he never broke the mower because he never borrowed it and anyway it was working when he gave it back, many Protestants deny that Catholics suffered disadvantage during the Stormont period, insist that, if they did, it was not because they were victims of discrimination but because they lacked some valuable property (such as self-discipline or diligence), and anyway, they deserved it because they would not support the state.

British government policy in Northern Ireland is seen by many Protestants as an affront and as a threat. As with the example of local authority powers, the British government has presented itself, and has often behaved, as a neutral umpire in the Northern

Ireland conflict. When the B Specials were judged to be partisan, the force was stood down and replaced by the Ulster Defence Regiment. Housing allocation was thought to be a problem, so it was taken from elected representatives and placed in the hands of an appointed professional and politically neutral body.[26] In much of its administration, the British government has tried to apply what it likes to think are particularly British principles of fair play. Indeed, this could even be described as the government's solution to the conflict. Divide legitimate minority grievances from illegitimate actions: resolve the former and control the latter. The affront is that, by recognizing that Catholics had cause for complaint and giving the power of redress to Westminster politicians and cosmopolitan civil servants, the government was announcing that Protestants behaved badly in the past and cannot be trusted to behave any better in the future.

One of the most important claims of the civil-rights movement was that Catholics were discriminated against in employment. Most loyalists do not accept the claim. They find it offensive that a supposedly impartial body such as the Cameron Commission— which was established by the government to investigate the cause of the 1969 disturbances—could accept the claim without any independent research.[27] They see the 'fair-employment' issue as a device to further nationalist interests under the disguise of equitable social policy: another stick to beat the Prods.

In 1976, four years after London took direct control of Northern Ireland, the Fair Employment Act was passed and the Fair Employment Agency (FEA) created. There then followed a decade of criticism that the FEA was a toothless body incapable of redressing decades of discrimination. There was also considerable pressure from the Irish–US lobby for the British government to adopt the 'MacBride Principles', which were modelled on rules drawn up for the employment practices of US companies working in South Africa. Some of these statements in favour of equal opportunity in the workplace are unexceptional. The first, for example, called for 'Increasing the representation of individuals from under-represented religious groups in the workforce, including managerial, supervisory, administrative, clerical and technical jobs'.[28] The main reasons they were resisted by the British government were fears that they would reduce inward investment, dislike for the politics of the people who most heavily promoted them (for example, Father McManus and the Irish National Caucus), and dislike for the implied parallel between Northern Ireland and South Africa. Although the government did not seem much moved by this particular section, many Ulster loyalists were annoyed by the third principle, which called for the 'banning of provocative religious and political emblems from the workplace'. The difficulty, of course, lies in the word 'provocative'. Symbols which Americans would regard as required marks of patriotism (the national flag, for example) in the Ulster context can be 'offensive'. Those American minorities whose equal opportunities might be in need of protection (blacks or hispanics, for example) are not disputing the constitutional position of the United States and thus do not object to the flying of the US flag. Or, in so far as some do, nobody takes them seriously, and some Congressmen want to make it a criminal offence to insult the flag by, for example, burning it. In Ulster, flying the Union Jack can be interpreted by Irish nationalists as provocation and intimidation. Although the MacBride Principles were not accepted, the British government did move to strengthen its policies. In 1989 there was a second Fair Employment Act and the FEA was reconstituted with increased powers as the Fair Employment Commission.

A difficulty for social engineering is that, even if every individual with power and influence now behaved with impeccable impartiality, this would not remedy the considerable socio-economic disparities. Although social structures do change, they do so very slowly because parents pass on to their children their advantages. In the world of middle-class work, a well-to-do family reproduces its class position by ensuring, by paying for it if necessary, that its children are well educated and gain the best credentials so that they can secure the same class position. For the working class, personal contacts can ensure that information about opportunities circulates best among those who already have them. Furthermore, in a divided society people tend to draw on the services of members of their own ethnic group. So Protestants who need solicitors, accountants, and doctors will favour

Protestant solicitors, accountants, and doctors. The more affluent an ethnic group, the more of such work there is.

There may also be characteristics of Catholics that retard their social mobility, irrespective of the behaviour of Protestants. Large family size may reproduce poverty. The curriculum of Catholic schools produces fewer school-leavers with science qualifications and hence fewer graduates trained in science and technology subjects.[29] Add those characteristics to the inertia effect of families in any social system passing on to their children their advantages and disadvantages and it becomes obvious that simply outlawing further discrimination does little to redress historical imbalances.

The US response in the context of racial disadvantage was to promote 'affirmative action', which often took the form of positive discrimination in favour of the previously unfavoured. British legislation does not permit this, because it is inherently unfair to punish individual members of a group that is on aggregate privileged when the individuals themselves may be as deprived as members of the minority group (and US law has shifted against positive discrimination). However, decisions can be taken on apparently 'universalistic' grounds (decentralizing government, for example) which have obvious sectarian consequences. In June 1993 it was announced that Civil Service jobs were to be transferred from Belfast and Bangor to Derry and Downpatrick. The public service union NIPSA announced that it was in favour of an active policy of correcting the imbalance of jobs.[30] That can be seen as an entirely justified response to decades of over-investment in Protestant areas. Whatever our moral or political response, we cannot escape the fact that such a policy has sectarian consequences in that the fortunes of individuals are still being determined by their ethnic identity, only the shoe is now on the other foot. The dependence of the economy on foreign investment allows further redistribution of wealth as firms which work for US companies are pressed by the Irish-American lobby to favour firms with a Catholic work-force.[31]

In a declining economy, the sectarian consequences of any genuinely redistributive employment policy would be even greater, because it is not enough to give all new jobs to Catholics. Protestants would have to be displaced from their jobs and replaced with Catholics. Again, we may think that quite appropriate. However, the effect would be to benefit more Catholic individuals than Protestant individuals, and, in a situation of ethnic conflict, that will always be read as benefiting the Catholic people at the expense of the Protestant people. As an article in the UDA-related magazine *New Ulster Defender* put it: 'If the job situation does not improve and if the unemployment figures remain at the same level, how is it possible to place more Catholics in jobs other than by displacing Protestants from the positions they now hold or by impeding Protestants from gaining employment at the present rate?'[32]

At the risk of labouring the point, three additional observations should be made to illustrate the strength of opposition to government employment policies. First, the security forces (taken in the broadest sense to include civilian searchers, the Prison Service, and people who provide services for the forces) provide an important source of employment in the province. Perhaps £600m. of the £1.4 billion annual subvention of Northern Ireland is spent on security. For their own reasons (either because they have political reasons to boycott such work or because they fear reprisals from those who would see such work boycotted), few Catholics are willing to work in this sector. With Catholics unwilling to consider a large sector of well-paid employment, for both groups to enjoy apparently equitable shares of the rest of the work available Catholics would actually have to have a far larger than proportionate share. Protestants do not think that is fair.

Secondly, unionists believe Catholic fertility to be higher than their own. This means that, just to stand still, to keep the disparities at their present levels, there must be a considerable preference for Catholics and hence any redress means considerable costs to Protestants.

Thirdly, rightly or wrongly, many unionists believe that the FEC is only interested in settings where Catholics are a minority. They argue that Catholics behave in a thoroughly discriminatory manner when they get the chance. According to Gregory Campbell of the DUP, the FEC's own figures show that the

three large companies in Northern Ireland with the worst record
(in the sense of hiring the fewest of whichever group is the
minority) are Catholic firms in Newry, Fermanagh, and Derry.
The Newry firm has a work-force of 370 and only ten Protestants;
the Fermanagh firm has 285 workers, only ten of whom are
Protestant. The Derry firm, located at the edge of the strongly
nationalist Creggan estate, has fewer than ten Protestants in a
work-force of over 700.

Many of the people I interviewed offered their own examples
of Catholics doing exactly what the Prods were supposed to have
done. To cite one case that was widely reported, a suitably
qualified Protestant woman claimed that she had been unfairly
passed over for the post of Chief Executive for Cookstown
District Council; a Catholic was appointed. The UUP and
independent unionists supported a male Protestant candidate, the
four DUP councillors the Protestant woman, and the six SDLP
councillors and one Sinn Fein member were able to appoint the
Catholic man. Asked by a Fair Employment tribunal if such
voting along party lines was not a 'remarkable coincidence', the
former town clerk said: 'for a town clerk in Northern Ireland it's
not surprising.'[33]

Of course, my Protestant respondents might be citing such
cases and arguing that Catholics are as bad as Protestants if not
worse because they wish to avoid feeling guilty about the way
that the old Stormont regime treated the minority. However, I
suspect that the main cause of Protestants' hostility to fair-
employment legislation is that they do not believe that a fair
liberal democracy is possible in the Irish context. The world is so
radically divided that any social policy, no matter how fine-
sounding in principle, must be to someone's detriment, and now
it is the Prods who are getting it in the ear.

In many of my interviews a more subtle complaint came to the
surface. As part of a lengthy comparison of Protestant virtues and
Catholics vices, one loyalist business man said: 'We don't hold
our hands out all the time expecting that the world owes us a
living.' In part this is merely a restatement of long-held
assumptions about the beneficial consequences of Protestantism
with its stress on self-reliance and individual responsibility.

Although few evangelicals will have read the German sociologist Max Weber's essay on 'The Protestant Ethic and the Spirit of Capitalism',[34] many have absorbed a popularized version of the thesis that reformed religion had the secondary consequence of promoting a 'this-worldly' asceticism. Where the medieval monk demonstrated his religious calling by retreating from the world (hence 'other-worldly' asceticism), the post-Reformation puritan glorified God by working hard in his mundane calling. Diligently laying bricks was as pleasing to God as a life of self-denial in a monastery. At the height of the Protestant crusades of the nineteenth century this claimed link between religion and civic virtue was developed into a vicious parody of the diligent, temperate, and honest Protestant and the gin-soaked, gambling, feckless Catholic. It is not surprising, given the continuing ethnic conflict in Ireland, that such stereotypes should continue to be common, but the above quotation suggests that there is something more than the trading of invidious caricatures going on here.

Although one would need a considerable amount of good research to pursue this point, I suspect that *petit bourgeois* Ulster Protestants are sensing, though they are not yet fully articulating, a general tide in the development of modern economies (especially not very successful ones) that they are ill suited to catch. First, a basic feature of modern capitalism is that an ever smaller proportion of the work-force is needed for material production, which leaves an ever-larger number of people to work in administration and other forms of white-collar work.[35] Secondly, the growth of the welfare state has meant that much white-collar work has been concerned with government and public administration rather than private manufacturing, retail, or service enterprise. Thirdly, especially in the disadvantaged inner-city areas and margins of modern economies, an increasing amount of work is being provided by tax-payers' money being channelled into economic regeneration schemes. The 1994 European Union 'Objective-1' funding programme is one such scheme. Well-paid jobs are being created not by traditional wealth-creating means in manufacture or distribution but by governmental and related agencies funding various 'programmes'. The major benefit of such schemes is seen, not by the working class (few permanent real jobs are created), but by the new middle class which devises and administers the programmes. These jobs are going, not to the people with the traditional skills of turning a profit, generating capital, and investing it to make further profits, but to articulate college graduates with skills in writing programme proposals, addressing funding meetings, and cultivating the right politicians. The typical Free Presbyterian knows how to run the family farm or small chain of shops. He does not know how to bid to the International Fund for Ireland and he is resentful of those who do. It might well be that an 'unfair' proportion of tax-payers' money is being spent in predominantly Catholic areas, but there is a more general point that late capitalist economies no longer need the 'Protestant ethic'.

It is interesting that class divisions within the Protestant community surface over the issue of 'holding out the hand'. A community worker in a deprived Protestant area of Belfast interrupted a Protestant business man who was complaining to me about the apparent skills of Catholics at collecting welfare benefits to insist that 'well, it's about time the Prods learnt to get their share'. His reaction was not to fault Catholics in deprived areas for making the best of what could be had from the government and European Union but to castigate his fellow Protestants for not better making their case. A very obvious problem is that the run-down of the traditional heavy industries which used to provide high-paid and steady work for the Protestant working class has removed a major source of a sense of superiority over Catholics, but, rather than see this as a world-wide economic trend quite unrelated to the conflict in Northern Ireland, many Protestants place it in the context of a zero-sum game; if we are losing, it must be because Catholics are gaining.

Loyalist dislike for government social policy is reinforced by the political goal of reducing Catholic support for Sinn Fein and the IRA. Despite the regular denials of a link between deprivation and crime in the British context, the government has long believed that economic development in nationalist areas will reduce the strength of the republican movement. To the secular loyalist, this is the state subsidizing republican terrorists: 'Kill enough policemen and the government will give your area lots of money to persuade you not to kill more!' The evangelical has an additional objection. In order to prevent tax-payers' money falling into the hands of republican groups, the government has chosen to direct much of its funding through the Catholic Church. Interestingly, loyalists here find Catholic support for their complaints. At a conference of Protestant and Catholic Belfast community workers held in 1992:

Church control of ACE schemes was mentioned as a problem by both communities but particularly within the Catholic community. Conference participants pointedly expressed the Catholic community's real sense of resentment and betrayal at the way their church dominated ACE work. The Catholic church leaders were accused of being more interested in 'control' rather than genuine economic development.[36]

To the evangelical Protestant, this is the state rewarding the spokesmen for the Anti-Christ.

PROTESTANT SELF-CONFIDENCE

It is very hard to generalize about a whole population of people from one person's experience of even a large number of them, and the more subtle the concern, the more difficult is the generalization, but in a lot of my interviews I sensed a deep fear that was barely articulated but is worth some examination: a sense of inadequacy. One loyalist, in complaining about what he perceived to be the anti-unionist bias of the mass media, said: 'When did you last hear a Roman Catholic who was not able to put his case well or a Protestant who was?' Contrast that with the images of Catholics presented by working-class periodicals such as *Loyalist News*, produced in the early 1970s by John McKeague, the founder of the Red Hand Commando. Here crude cartoons and jokes constantly present Catholics (and especially IRA men) as very stupid, drunken, and unwashed, and the women as slatternly. Add a third image. A leading UVF man talking about his childhood on the lower Shankill Road spoke with considerable resentment of constantly being told about the underprivileged Catholics, when Catholic children walked past his house in their neat school uniforms on their way to a decent education which would lead them to places at the Queen's University. The best he and his people could hope for when they left school at 15 was a job in the shipyards.

There are, of course, exceptions, but until the 1960s Protestants were raised to think of themselves as superior. In so far as Protestants saw themselves as having advantages, then they merited them. Catholics were a joke. Their political leaders—the old Nationalists in Stormont—were 'couthy buddies'. Their country was backward, their industry non-existent, and their farming hopelessly antiquated. If they had charms, they were the charms of children. The late 1960s saw those comfortable stereotypes brutally challenged. Apparently out of nowhere, the Catholic minority acquired skilled articulate young politicians. Gerry Fitt and Paddy Devlin may have been in the old mould, but John Hume and Austin Currie and Bernadette Devlin and Gerry Adams were young and clever and they knew how to court public opinion. Because the Protestants had been raised to see Catholics as no real threat, when the Catholics began successfully to pursue their own interests, the response of many unionists was not to see this as battle fairly joined but as the Catholics *cheating*. They had no right to put their case so well.

Either the Catholics were cheating or everyone was on their side. Hence the accusations of media bias. Loyalists fell easily into a self-pitying assumption that the world was against them. In the words of a chant used by a number of football fans: 'Nobody loves us and we don't care!' But beneath that, many loyalists seem to be harbouring a lurking suspicion that perhaps the Catholics are not so stupid after all. Perhaps the loyalists have been misled.

Jackie Redpath, a community worker on the Shankill for twenty-five years, said something similar in his submission to the Opsahl Commission. In a reporter's summary:

Protestants . . . were ashamed of their heritage, afflicted with lack of confidence, and in physical and cultural retreat. He told of one community worker who finally 'came out of the closet' as a Protestant by changing her name; all her friends had assumed she was Catholic because she seemed 'all right'. Poets and writers rubbished the culture and many refused to admit they were Protestants. Catholics, on the other hand, seemed 'ascendant, going somewhere, on the move'.[37]

TRUST AND THE BRITISH GOVERNMENT

Since the start of the Troubles and direct London interest in the province, there have been some who have seen British policy as having the goal of reneging on the deal of 1920 and giving the North to the Irish Republic. The introduction of direct rule in 1972, the imposition of the Sunningdale agreement with its power-sharing Executive and the Council of Ireland in 1974, the negotiations with the IRA, the clear desire of London to placate the Irish lobby in US politics: unionists readily see all of these as evidence that the British government does not extend to its citizens in Northern Ireland the same rights and protections that it extends to citizens in Glasgow and Birmingham.

Although every year since 1970 has seen the numbers of those sceptical of British policy increase, the Anglo-Irish inter-governmental agreement of November 1985 dramatically changed unionist perceptions. Prime Minister Margaret Thatcher and Taoiseach Garret Fitzgerald met at Hillsborough Castle to sign an agreement which repeated the usual bromides about working together for peace and stability in Northern Ireland and then announced a genuinely radical innovation. The agreement established

a joint ministerial conference of British and Irish ministers, backed by a permanent secretariat at Maryfield, close to the Stormont estate, to monitor political, security, legal and other issues of concern to the Nationalist minority. Thus, while the agreement was not formally a joint authority, since the UK government had the final word on matters affecting NI, it represented a major change of attitude by the British PM.[38]

Despite the reassuring noises made to them by the British

government, unionists saw the granting to the Republic of an institutionalized channel for 'interference' in the affairs of Ulster as an unambiguous sign that Northern Ireland was being pushed out of the United Kingdom. Furthermore, that the agreement came out of the blue made many unionists conclude that the British government simply could not be trusted. Only three years earlier Thatcher had rudely dismissed similar proposals made by the New Ireland Forum, and, though John Hume and the SDLP had been kept thoroughly briefed in the build-up to the accord by Dublin civil servants, no unionist representatives had any inkling of the negotiations.

Irrespective of the specific content of the accord (and that, with its Dublin role, was bad enough), the logic underlying it was deeply offensive and threatening. The master stroke of the accord was that, unlike the Sunningdale agreement, it did not require the active participation of unionists. It was solely a compact between London and Dublin. As there was nothing to boycott, and hence no possibility of withdrawing consent, it could not be scuppered, and it signalled that, as far as London was concerned, unionists were of no account. Worse, it meant that unionists were of less account than nationalists because the accord was devised in consultation with the SDLP, and it enshrined the voice of the constitutional nationalists through their Dublin representatives. Ironically, of Eire politicians it is Proinsias de Rossa, the leader of the Democratic Left (the heir to the political front of the Official IRA), who most forcefully warned against the ethnic-interest nature of the Republic's involvement in the North when he said 'the Dublin government should stop seeing its role in structures of the Anglo-Irish agreement solely in terms of defending the interest of northern Catholics. This was a sectarian approach which only confirmed unionist suspicions of north–south links.'[39]

Rather than take the view desired by unionists that the state should see itself as the protector of those of its citizens who are loyal to it, the British state has often presented itself as a neutral party. To give a few recent examples, in December 1992 Mayhew described the government's role in the then constitutional talks as a 'facilitator' with no independent political agenda.[40] More damagingly, in an interview with the German magazine *Die Zeit*, he said: 'Many people believe that we would not want to release Northern Ireland from the United Kingdom. To be entirely honest—with pleasure.' He immediately backtracked and added: 'No, not with pleasure, I take that back', and then repeated the orthodox line: 'But we would not stand in the way of Northern Ireland, if that would be the will of the majority.' However, that he strongly hoped it was the will of the majority was made clear when he went on to say: 'The province costs us three billion pounds per year. Three billion pounds for one and a half million people.'[41] Hardly the remarks to reassure nervous unionists. A leading UVF man told me: 'Mayhew says the British have no economic or political interest in Northern Ireland. Well, they bloody well should have, because we are still British citizens.'

Although some loyalists (especially in the UDA and UVF) are very critical of the Stormont regime and accept that unionists could have done more to persuade Catholics to become loyal citizens, all loyalists and the vast majority of unionists see republicanism as the cause of the present conflict. The British state is being attacked by the IRA. The only appropriate response is for the British state to defend its citizens. Anything else is appeasement; pointless at best and at worse positively dangerous, because, as Hitler's career shows, trying to buy off the bully merely encourages his appetite. In the ideal imagined world of loyalists and unionists, the constitutional position of Northern Ireland would be no more discussed than was the constitutional position of Britain in 1939. The government would just get on with its job of putting down a rebellion. Against that template of what is desired by loyalists, pretty well anything the government does is a betrayal.

There is a nervous strand in unionism that has never been confident of the permanency of the partition settlement. Ian Paisley is merely the last in a long line of loyalists calling the people to be wary of the intentions of their political masters. One way of interpreting Paisley's political success is to say that with each passing year more and more unionists have become persuaded of his political analysis; what was dismissed as paranoia in the early 1960s is now seen as prescience. In an impassioned speech at Westminster against the Anglo-Irish accord, made all the more poignant by his terminal illness, Unionist MP Harold McCusker, who had long been regarded as a moderate man, spoke of his shame at having been so contemptuously ignored by his government. That sense is now as likely to inform the editorials of the staid *Ulster News Letter* as the pages of *Combat* and the *Burning Bush*.[42] To cite just one example, in May 1993 the *Ulster News Letter* commented on the above ministerial speeches that the government's commitment to Northern Ireland 'is a flexible commitment, its strength depending almost entirely on the political views and aspirations of the audience being addressed'.[43]

In most of my talks with loyalists, conversation got around to the British government's 'guarantee' to unionists and the difficulties of explaining to outsiders (which would include the British government!) why unionists were not reassured. As this is central to much unionist thinking, it is worth dwelling on. The Northern Ireland Constitution Act of 1973 says: 'It is hereby declared that Northern Ireland remains part of Her Majesty's Dominions and of the United Kingdom, and it is hereby affirmed that in no event will Northern Ireland or any part of it cease to be part of Her Majesty's Dominions and of the United Kingdom without the consent of the majority of the people of Northern Ireland voting in a poll held for the purpose.' In the early days of the Troubles, the British assertion that Northern Ireland would remain British so long as that was the will of the majority seemed like a solid promise, and the fears of the nervous were concerned with whether or not they meant it. In 1985 unionists were encouraged by the government to take heart from the fact that the same promise was repeated in the introduction to the Anglo-Irish accord and was thus now accepted by the government of the Irish Republic. However, the increase in the Catholic proportion of the population has changed what was a promise into a threat. Paisley does not think a Catholic majority will come in his lifetime, but it is conceivable that within thirty years two-thirds of local councils will have nationalist majorities. What if they all voted to leave the United Kingdom? It is possible that a devolved assembly might have a Catholic majority. What if it voted to leave the United Kingdom? What would the British government do then?

It is the contemplation of that position which has alerted unionists to an apparent unfairness in the position of the British government. In every test of public opinion—Westminster elections, European elections, council elections, opinion polls— there has to date been a clear and large 'unionist' majority in the sense that either unionist parties have won a majority of votes or a majority of expressions of opinion has been in favour of continuing with the British link. And that unionist majority has included a large number of Catholics. Yet this clear 'will of the majority' has always been dismissed as insufficient because it does not do enough to satisfy radical nationalist opinion and hence to produce a stable political settlement. For very sensible reasons, in a divided society with a considerable minority unwilling to commit itself to the active support of the institutions of the status quo, majoritarianism is not acceptable. Yet that same logic is not applied to the possible future in which the roles of majority and minority are reversed. The government is committed to accepting the 'will of the majority' if and when it sounds for a radical break. As it appears to many unionists, a unionist majority is not a majority but a nationalist majority will be!

The Anglo-Irish accord has created the framework within which loyalists now interpret every salient event in their world. The pressure to redistribute resources from Protestant areas to Catholic areas, fair-employment legislation, the re-routing of Orange parades away from Catholic areas of Northern Ireland, the Stevens inquiry into security-force collusion with loyalist paramilitaries—all these are seen as Dublin's doing, as is the heavy-handed policing of loyalists suspected of paramilitary involvement. Among the graffiti that appeared on walls in the Shankill after rioting in July 1993 was 'RUC—paid in punts'. Finally, the unprecedented granting in August 1993 of permission for a nationalist anti-internment rally in the centre of Belfast was cited by everyone to whom I talked as evidence that Dublin's hand was working the puppet glove of British administration in Northern Ireland.

It is one of life's great ironies that all the recent significant changes in the position of Northern Ireland have been produced by Conservative governments. That party used to be called the Conservative and Unionist Party.[44] Ulster Unionists took the Conservative whip at Westminster and held junior ministerial office in Conservative governments. What of the alternative? Loyalists can find little comfort in contemplating a Labour government. Although Labour in office has always been a better friend to the unionists than the party's stated policy implies, it is a long time since a Labour government and in the interim the party's left wing (explicitly nationalist and sometimes friendly towards Sinn Fein) has acquired more influence. Though Kevin McNamara, a consistent critic of Sinn Fein and supporter of the SDLP, holds the Northern Ireland portfolio, it is still remembered that Ken Livingston is a Labour MP and Livingston has frequently been willing to appear on platforms with Gerry Adams. Unionist fears were confirmed in July 1993 when a Labour party consultation document on Northern Ireland was leaked.[45] It proposed that the parties in Northern Ireland be given six months to come to agreement. If they did not, then London and Dublin should negotiate joint control, regardless of local opposition. This was proposed without any honest recognition that such a default system was profoundly one-sided in that it overrode the veto of only one side in the local dispute: the unionists. It would give every advantage to the SDLP, which would only have to stonewall until the six-month period was up, when it would get something much closer to its desires than the present system. Although the idea had the superficial ring of fairness, it was simply a nationalist project. The document further suggested that the Irish President Mary Robinson and the Queen should be joint heads of state. One of my respondents nailed the absurdity perfectly when he found the following silver lining: 'They could overprint Robinson's head on the Queen's on the stamps, like they did during the war in occupied territories in the far east. Fuck all use as politics but a bloody stamp collector's dream!'

At the same time, a Labour paper on the possibility of recruiting and organizing in Northern Ireland was leaked to the press. As well as reasserting that Labour was in favour of a united Ireland, it argued that fielding candidates in Ulster would take votes from the SDLP, which, according to the authors, would be a bad thing.[46]

When I suggested to a senior UVF man that this was of really no consequence because Labour lost the election, he pointed out that they did not lose by much and might not lose the next time!

It is extremely easy to summarize the loyalist view of British governments of the Troubles: fools, knaves, or both. When all else is said and done, most British governments have not believed in the Union. The emotional commitment has not been there and everything else is just politics, and the general drift of those politics has been to appease republicans in the North and the Republic.

WATCHING THE DARK

If we are interested in some large population, our research must always involve sampling. We cannot interview all Ulster Protestants. There is always a balance to be struck between depth and spread. The survey can gather superficial information about very large numbers of people; the lengthy conversation provides considerable insight into the minds of a small number. In the end, as it says on cereal-packet competitions, 'skill and judgement' have to be used to estimate just how typical are the views that have been gathered and how far they can be generalized.

I began by noting the central division among Ulster Protestants between Ulster loyalists and Ulster British. The former see themselves primarily in terms of their 'Ulster-ness' while the latter are 'West Britons'. To a large extent those distinctions map on to class divisions. The professional middle classes may well have studied in Britain or abroad, may well have worked in another country at some point in their careers, are much closer in beliefs and values to the modern western European norms (tending to the liberal, sexually permissive, and secular), and have little difficulty finding a home, psychological as well as material, in Great Britain. The characteristics that give them high status, personal wealth, and professional skills are transferable.[47] As though hoping to fool themselves into believing they are already somewhere else, the residents of Holywood, County Down, name their streets after places in Scotland: Strathearn Court, Rannoch Drive, Lochinver Avenue. But the working classes, the small farmers, the small business men, they have nowhere else to go. Their identity and their sense of self-worth are firmly located in the history and geography of Northern Ireland. If they move to England or Scotland to work, as many do, far from carrying their high status as loyal diligent citizens of the power house of the British Empire, they are seen as humourless bigots, or worse, they are taken for 'Paddies'.

The interests of the Ulster British insulate them to a certain extent from the conflict and reduce it to a nuisance. It may be a painful nuisance, but it does not go to the heart of their sense of place in the world. No such distancing is possible for the Ulster loyalist, because what is at stake is everything. It is just possible for an Ulster unionist to view the last twenty-five years in a cheerful light. Despite everything, Northern Ireland is still part of the United Kingdom. Although the IRA continues to murder, the security forces enjoy considerable success in bringing terrorists to book and in preventing atrocities. There is a simmering civil war, but, compared to Bosnia or South Africa, Northern Ireland is peaceful; in the South African townships hundreds of people are murdered every month. Those in work continue to enjoy a decent standard of living and, for some of the time, life goes on as normal. The British government, especially when it needs the votes of Ulster Unionist MPs to sustain it in office (as it did in July 1993), sometimes makes strongly unionist noises. Such equanimity is more common among the Ulster British and the cosmopolitan middle classes than it is among the Ulster loyalists, who, for all the reasons described in this chapter, see the period of the Troubles as a journey from good to bad or from bad to worse.

3. TALKS

THE previous chapter was intended to explain what the world now looks like to working-class loyalists, to the unionists of the DUP, and to an increasing number of Ulster Protestants beyond those two circles. I now want to examine in some detail the political situation of the period from 1991 to the end of 1993—a time when the increasing tempo of political murder stimulated a revival of political debates and initiatives.

Since 1986 the British government has been looking for some internal progress in Northern Ireland to complement the Anglo-Irish accord and to break the deadlock of the unionist boycott. In 1988 Secretary of State Tom King held a series of meetings with party leaders to talk about what it would take to make them talk. These were continued by King's successor, Peter Brooke. Despite the SDLP being none too keen to negotiate an alternative to the accord and the unionists refusing to talk except in the context of replacing the hated agreement, the parties agreed to begin formal talks in the spring of 1991.

To everyone's surprise, the UDA and UVF issued a joint statement (in the name of the Combined Loyalist Military Command) announcing that: 'In the light of impending political dialogue and in common with the sincere and genuine desire to see a peaceful and acceptable solution to our political differences, the combined commands of all loyalist paramilitary organisations shall order a universal suspension of aggressive operational hostilities commencing midnight of the night preceding the political summit.' The paramilitaries were very nearly wasting their breath. Brooke's skill in leading the parties to the table despite themselves seems to have had a lot to do with fudging and dodging issues. At the last minute, arguments about the locations of the various strands of talks threatened to derail them, as did an argument about the chairman for the 'strand-2' negotiations (which would be concerned with North–South relations). Unionists were horrified when Brooke suggested Lord Carrington as the chairman. Brooke either did not know or did not care that Carrington was on record as calling Paisley 'the bigot of all bigots' and was thought by unionists to have been involved in negotiations with the IRA when he was Minister of Defence in the early 1970s. But finally venues were agreed and Sir Ninian Stephens, a prominent Australian lawyer and politician, was invited to chair the discussions and they got under way.

The size of the gulf between the parties was immediately clear from the negotiating-position papers they submitted at the start. The SDLP's spoke warmly of the Anglo-Irish accord, was heavy on the need to recognize the 'Irish dimension', and wanted any devolution of powers to Northern Ireland to be set firmly within the context of the 'totality' of Anglo-Irish relations. It was also keen on European involvement and critical of security policy. The two Unionist submissions agreed in being opposed to Dublin involvement, but otherwise disagreed, with Paisley's DUP being in favour of devolution while Molyneaux's UUP tended towards further integration with Britain. Six weeks after they started, the talks ended, when the British and Irish governments insisted on holding a scheduled meeting of the inter-governmental conference.

Almost everyone blamed the failure on the unionists. The editor of *Fortnight*[1] seemed largely alone in supposing that the SDLP's happiness with the accord made it a reluctant negotiator. The BBC's Panorama, with a film called *No Surrender, No Progress*, set the tone for most responses by pointing to unionist intransigence. Protestant church leaders were highly critical of unionist politicians. Church of Ireland Primate Bishop Robin Eames talked of 'missed opportunities' and looked for 'other aspiring politicians who could come into the talks process' and take up where Paisley and Molyneaux had left off.[2] A former Moderator of the Presbyterian Church made the same point.

First the probability and then the event of a British general election delayed any attempt to resume talks until early 1992, when, under the direction of the new Secretary of State Sir Patrick Mayhew, the parties once again sat down.

This time there was substantial progress in the strand of talks concerned with the government of Northern Ireland. Both unionist parties, the Alliance Party, and the British government agreed on a complex structure of committees elected from an assembly. Since 1974 unionists have been formally opposed to institutionalized 'power-sharing' on the grounds that it enshrines the sectarian divide and gives the SDLP more power than it is due. So much effort was put into opposing Sunningdale that even those who now favoured the reality of power-sharing had to avoid the plague carried by the phrase. Among the significant departures from old scripts was the DUP's frank recognition that a return to the old majority-rule cabinet of Stormont (and Westminster, it must be remembered) was not possible. Indeed, as though better to persuade doubters that he was sincere, Paisley was keen to point out that a majoritarian system would hurt his party, because it is smaller than the UUP. In his opening statement, he said:

these talks cannot bring back the old Stormont. Many on the unionist side might understandably long for the pre-1972 Stormont set-up, but our delegations at this table realise, as the representatives of the unified unionist electorate, that this is not attainable. . . . I am not afraid as a unionist to admit that the old Stormont system had its faults. . . . The Ulster Democratic Unionist Party had no part in government under the Stormont system and none of my colleagues from the Ulster Unionist Party at this table today served in any Stormont government either. So although in many ways it may be unpalatable to the majority unionist people of this province that we cannot press for nor attain a pre-1972 Stormont, yet realistically the unionist population have faced up to the fact. We are not here to talk about something that is beyond our reach.[3]

As power-sharing could not be mentioned, something very similar was arrived at through the negative process of preventing the majority party in the elected assembly exercising unfettered control. In addition to a series of leaderless committees, there would be three 'commissioners' elected from outside the assembly. This element was introduced to placate the SDLP.

John Hume would not accept an executive that was directly and democratically elected by the assembly; that would not guarantee the SDLP the power it sought for itself as the representative of the 'nationalist people'. He wanted a six-man executive, of whom three would be directly elected (and, if one takes the European elections as the model, that would give one each to the SDLP, the UUP, and the DUP) and the other three would be appointed by Dublin, London, and the European Community. The other parties accepted the idea of commissioners but would not accept that any of them should be appointed, and especially not from outside Northern Ireland or the United Kingdom.

Thus in strand 1 there was agreement by all the Ulster parties except the SDLP, which could agree only 'with reservations' about the mode of election and the nature of the commissioners; that is, it could not agree.

As was predictable, the strand-2 talks—North and South— made very little headway. The ambition of the SDLP and the Dublin government representatives was to increase Dublin's say in the North or at least to fix it at the influence it had through the Anglo-Irish accord. The unionists wanted the accord scrapped and links between North and South reduced to the cordial relations between separate states, promised by all sides in an agreement signed in 1925 but never attained. In particular they wanted the Dublin government to remove or at least to discuss the removal of Articles 2 and 3 from de Valera's 1937 constitution of the Republic. Article 1 says: 'The Irish nation hereby affirms its inalienable, indefeasible, and sovereign right to choose its own form of government, to determine its relations with other nations, and to develop its life, political, economic and cultural, in accordance with its own genius and traditions.' This might seem unobjectionable, except that the history of the Republic has made it clear that many Irish people take the 'genius' to be thoroughly Roman Catholic. Article 2 states: 'The national territory consists of the whole island of Ireland, its islands and the territorial seas.' In other words, the Republic claims Northern Ireland.

Unionists see Dublin's claim to the North not just as a

symbolic affront but as one cause of the violence. So long as the Republic asserts that it owns Northern Ireland, its condemnation of republican terrorism will ring false and the IRA will continue to take heart from knowing that its view of Northern Ireland is still the formal position of the twenty-six counties. For many years, any reference to Articles 2 and 3 was seen as proof of being a paranoid Paisleyite. Encouraged by Dublin politicians who wanted to play the green card at home and the moderate abroad, many commentators and British and Ulster politicians took the view that the articles were vague statements of aspiration, not to be taken too seriously. However, two leading Unionists saw in them an opportunity to embarrass Dublin over the Anglo-Irish accord, which begins by acknowledging that Northern Ireland shall remain British so long as that is what most people want. The McGimpsey brothers asked the Dublin Supreme Court to rule that the Irish government could not endorse the accord because such an admission defied the Irish constitution. Although it did nothing to weaken the accord, the Court did agree that Articles 1 and 2 were statements of realistic policy and not vague hopes. This ruling meant that unionists now had a stick with which to beat Dublin and, more importantly, a clear negotiating target. A new relationship with the Republic would be possible only when it recognized the place of Ulster in the United Kingdom and gave up its territorial claims.

The strand-2 talks quickly got bogged down in arguments about the order in which the various items for discussion should be taken, but the procedural disputes were only a way of expressing the fundamental differences of purpose between the unionist and nationalist parties. The wrangling continued until the talks were brought to a halt by an imminent meeting of the Anglo-Irish inter-governmental conference. As in the first round of talks, the British and Dublin governments had tactfully delayed meetings of the conference to allow the unionists to participate in talks despite their opposition to the accord, but, presumably because they could see that resolution was not close at hand, the British government announced that the November 1992 meeting of the conference would take place and hence the constitutional talks closed.

Two big things came out of the Mayhew talks. First, the finger-pointing shifted from the unionists to the SDLP. Secondly, as details of what had and had not been agreed filtered out, it became clear that the SDLP was asking for something which unionists could not deliver while remaining unionists.

THE PAN-NATIONALIST FRONT

Crucial in the subsequent hardening of unionist perceptions of the SDLP's position were the discussions that John Hume held with Gerry Adams, the leader of Sinn Fein, in early April 1993. In order to appreciate the significance of those talks, it is worth going back and briefly reviewing the origins of the Social Democratic and Labour Party.

The SDLP came out of the civil-rights movement and the desire of younger nationalists to replace the moribund Nationalist Party, which had worked itself into irrelevance by, on the one hand, remaining committed to old-fashioned Irish nationalism and, on the other, co-operating with the Stormont regime as an 'Uncle Tom' opposition in parliament. The SDLP was formed in 1970 by seven Stormont politicians who came from a wide variety of party backgrounds. Gerry Fitt was Republican Labour. John Hume, Ivan Cooper, and Paddy O'Hanlon were Independents. Austin Currie was a Nationalist but a very young one and untainted by his party's history of stagnation. Paddy Wilson was a Republican Labour senator and Paddy Devlin was an MP for the Northern Ireland Labour Party.[4] With Fitt and Devlin initially two of the most prominent figures, the SDLP presented itself as a left-of-centre party which would seek civil rights for all, a redistribution of wealth, and increased friendship and under-standing between North and South with a view to the eventual unity of the island through the consent of the majority of the people, in Northern Ireland and the Republic of Ireland.

There was always a tension between the nationalist and socialist wings. In 1972, in an interview with a Dublin radio station, John Hume made his own position very clear. He said there were three possible futures for discussion: total integration with Britain, a restructured North, or Irish unity. 'The only viable one is the last and that is what we should be negotiating, as of now.'[5] In 1977 Paddy Devlin was expelled for criticizing the party's lack of socialism, and in 1979, when the party refused to join a constitutional convention because the agenda was insufficiently broad, Gerry Fitt resigned, describing the party as 'green nationalist'.

Since he has taken over as leader, John Hume and his party have prospered. Hume himself has been extremely successful in Europe, in Dublin, and in the United States at courting international support for the nationalist cause and for the SDLP. Despite losing some electoral ground in the early 1980s when Sinn Fein was successful in capitalizing on sympathy for the hunger-strikers, the party added the Westminster seats of Newry and Mourne (Seamus Mallon) and South Down (Eddie McGrady) to Hume's Foyle seat and in 1991 Joe Hendron regained West Belfast from Sinn Fein's Gerry Adams. Predictably the success of Hume and the SDLP has provoked increased loyalist loathing and hostility. Retreating into self-pity, many loyalists contrast Hume's easy success in international high politics with the lack of international understanding for the unionist cause. Mallon especially, probably because he has a high profile in criticizing security-force operations on the border, is hated by loyalists.

Unionists had long been upset that the SDLP had been able to get away with pretending that it was something other than a nationalist party (witness the British Labour Party's fiction that Protestant socialists should join the SDLP), but they still saw a significant difference between the SDLP and Sinn Fein, the political front of the IRA: the former wanted to persuade unionists to accept a united Ireland; the latter was willing to bomb unionists into the free republic. Since the party was formed, there have been periodic meetings with the IRA. In January 1988 Hume began a series of discussions with Sinn Fein President Adams 'in an attempt to find common ground on the conditions for an all-Ireland settlement'.[6] Hume apparently claimed that, with the Anglo-Irish accord, Britain 'is now saying that she has no interest of her own in being here'.[7] Perhaps because Hume and Adams did not come to any agreement, the unionist response was muted, and the firm association of nationalism with republicanism did not become widespread. There were, of course, some loyalists who could not be bothered with the niceties of division within Irish nationalism, but even DUP members and the more thoughtful operators in the UDA and UVF distinguished between constitutional nationalists and republicans. One could talk to the latter but not the former.

But for many loyalists this distinction was blurred in early 1993 when Hume not only held talks with Adams but in a joint statement appeared to accept a crucial part of the rhetoric of republicanism. The two men announced:

In striving for that end [national reconciliation], we accept that an internal settlement is not a solution because it obviously does not deal with all the relationships at the heart of the problem. We accept that the Irish people as a whole have a right to national self-determination. This is the view shared by a majority of the people of this island, though not by all its people.[8]

The shift for Adams, if he was sincere, was the acceptance in the statement that 'a new agreement is only achievable and viable if it can earn and enjoy the allegiance of the different traditions on this island, by accommodating diversity and providing for national reconciliation'.[9] This seems to recognize that unionists exist and will have to be accommodated. The shift for Hume was the acceptance of the IRA claim that the Irish people have a right to 'national self-determination'. In classic unreformed nationalist fashion, such an expression takes for granted what is at the heart of the Ulster problem by making all the residents of Ireland part of the Irish nation, whether they like it or not.

Whatever Hume's motives in talking with Adams, the response (and not just from loyalists) was one of surprise and indignation. The *Belfast Telegraph* offered the following précis of the views of former Dublin minister and leading Dublin liberal Conor Cruise O'Brien:

The SDLP had become a party 'which is not above doing a deal with the accomplices of terrorists in order to gain a collective communal and sectarian advantage'. He believes the joint statement 'is intended to close the Catholic and nationalist ranks in the coming local elections. It should ensure that in constituencies where Protestants and Catholics are in roughly equal numbers, the seat is won by a Catholic candidate, whether SDLP or Sinn Fein'.[10]

As an afternoon paper which sells to both sides in Northern Ireland, the *Telegraph* has usually ploughed a moderate and ecumenical furrow (its chief political correspondent wrote a very sympathetic biography of John Hume). In terms far more temperate than were used by the loyalists I interviewed, one of its editorials neatly identified the worrisome aspect of the talks:

Secret bilateral talks, which exclude others deeply involved in what is being discussed, are always a risky exercise. They can so easily be misinterpreted, because it looks as if the two are pursuing a common cause, to the disadvantage of the rest. And when the two parties involved represent the vast bulk of the nationalists in Northern Ireland, with very different approaches to the political process, the effect is even more puzzling.[11]

The announcement in September 1993 that Martin McGuinness, widely regarded in the province as still being an active IRA leader, was now involved in the talks confirmed ever worst unionist fears.

The response of the loyalist paramilitaries was to announce that, by associating itself so clearly with the republican movement, the SDLP had joined a 'pan-nationalist front' and its leaders were now legitimate targets. The phrase, which the SDLP found deeply offensive, had actually originated with Sinn Fein. In November 1985, when the unionist MPs announced their intention to stage by-elections as a protest against the Anglo-Irish accord, Sinn Fein had proposed that it and the SDLP field agreed candidates: 'the proposed resignations from Westminster seats presented an opportunity for pan-nationalist unity.'[12]

Although no one I interviewed mentioned that text, the widespread supposition was that Hume and Adams were planning an electoral pact, not for the 1993 local elections mentioned by O'Brien, but for the next Westminster election. At present Catholic majorities in the Westminster constituencies of

Fermanagh and South Tyrone and Mid-Ulster do not produce nationalist MPs because Sinn Fein and the SDLP are splitting the vote. A tacit pact would give one to Sinn Fein and one to the SDLP and give the nationalists six seats to the Unionists' eleven instead of the present four to thirteen. Those who did not cite so specific an advantage none the less asserted that it just proved what they had always suspected: all nationalists are the same.

As critical of Hume's talks with Sinn Fein as Conor Cruise O'Brien was Prionsias de Rossa, the leader of the Democratic Left, who said that the joint Hume–Adam statement about national self-determination and the rejection of any internal solution was 'driving moderate unionists to despair. I would have hoped that all democrats would accept that it is not possible to achieve political arrangements on Northern Ireland over the heads of the one million unionists, and any attempt to by-pass them is simply a recipe for disaster.'[13]

With perfect timing, Dick Spring, the Republic's Deputy Prime Minister, then proposed precisely that. If the local parties could not agree—or more honestly, for this is what he meant, if the unionists did not cave in and accept the SDLP's programme— Dublin and London should negotiate their own solution.

What the two sets of government-led talks between 1991 and 1993 did was to consolidate and clarify both sides. Twenty years ago, and still ten years ago, it would have been hard to imagine the staid *Ulster News Letter* lining up behind Ian Paisley, but in an editorial in May 1993 it did exactly that when it replied on Paisley's behalf to the criticism of a Dublin politician that Paisley was not interested in a settlement: 'If [the critic] means a settlement which suits Dublin he is probably right. For in recent weeks it has become apparent that friendly overtures made by Dublin under the initial talks process initiative by Peter Brooke were merely intended to lure unionists into a cul-de-sac where all the signs pointed towards a strengthening of Dublin's role in Ulster's affairs.'[14]

SEASON OF MISTS: AUTUMN 1993

On 26 September 1993 John Hume delivered to the Dublin government the joint proposal that was the outcome of his talks with Adams. He then flew to the United States for a ten-day trade mission. There was considerable annoyance from many quarters: Paisley complained that Hume had apparently discussed his grand scheme with US politicians and Nelson Mandela but not felt it appropriate to share it with the people of Northern Ireland. The Dublin government at first seemed unclear whether it had received any document. The British government struck an aloof posture and said that if any proposals were forwarded by the Dublin government then of course they would be considered but until then it had no comment to make. There was talk of the SDLP and Fianna Fail (the party of Prime Minister Reynolds, which had for many years been hand-in-glove with Hume) now being 'on a collision course'.[15]

A month later the IRA added its distinctive contribution to the speculation. On 23 October a large bomb exploded in Frizell's fish shop on the Shankill Road at midday. Ten people were killed, one of them Thomas Begley, the young man who was planting the bomb. The Provisional IRA announced that the bomb had exploded prematurely. The target was a meeting of the west Belfast UDA, which had an office above the shop, and it had been intended that sufficient warning would be given to clear people from the shop but still trap the UDA leaders upstairs. The IRA also told journalists that the bomb had been intended particularly for the leader of the UDA on the lower Shankill, dubbed by the media 'Mad Dog'. He was widely believed to have been responsible for about twenty murders in the previous two years and there had been numerous attempts on his life. His recklessness and bravado had made him something of a hero to young working-class Protestants in the area (and something of a nuisance to older people, who disliked the way that he and his men lorded it over the district). It had also made him a prime target for the IRA in the Ardoyne, a Catholic enclave bordering on the lower Shankill. With every failed IRA attempt on his life, his stock went up.

As often happens, accounts soon proliferated, as people who like to believe they are 'in the know' started to exchange information and pass on gossip to journalists. One UDA brigadier, for reasons which no one can understand, told journalists that there had indeed been a meeting in progress in the office that morning but that it had finished shortly before the bomb. Actually there had been no such meeting. Had the IRA men been better informed, they might have known that 'Mad Dog' was fifteen miles away, visiting a friend in the Maze prison. Shankill loyalists immediately rejected the IRA's explanation that it had been a surgical strike gone wrong and instead took it for granted that this was a deliberate attempt to kill as many civilians as possible. Even if mass murder of Protestants was not the intention, it is certainly the case that to plant such a large bomb at midday on a crowded shopping street showed thorough disregard for civilians.

The loyalist paramilitaries divided. There were many people, especially in the UVF, who thought that the greatest advantage to be won from the atrocity would be to do nothing and allow the media to turn on the IRA. Questions were immediately asked about the sincerity of Gerry Adams's commitment to peace talks. When Adams was shown on television news film acting as a pall-bearer at Begley's funeral, there was widespread questioning of John Hume's wisdom in continuing his dialogue with Sinn Fein. The Belfast paper *Sunday Life* urged Hume 'to pull the plug before the SDLP is so tarnished with the brush of violent republicanism that its standing is damaged beyond repair'.[16] David McKittrick in the *Independent* thought that the SDLP–Sinn Fein talks were in serious trouble and suggested that the bomb raised the question of whether Adams could deliver the IRA.[17] With the pressure of the Shankill bomb on top of the mounting hostility in Dublin and London to Hume, it looked as if nationalists were fallible after all. As one Shankill loyalist later put it to me: 'For the first time in a long time not everything was going their fuckin' way. All we had to do was sit back and watch them fall out among themselves. Reynolds, Hume and Adams arguing amongst themselves for once.'

However, there were also those who argued that the sympathy

after previous atrocities (Enniskillen, for example) had made no difference to the IRA or to the government's general political direction and that what was needed was retaliation. Those voices won out in the UDA. The UFF announced that its members would be 'fully mobilized' and promised (notice the interesting order of names) that 'John Hume, Gerry Adams and the nationalist electorate will pay a heavy, heavy price for today's atrocity'.[18] A week after the Shankill Road bomb, the UFF retaliated and, as so often, the victims were not republicans or even nationalist activists but ordinary civilians. A Belfast council cleansing depot was shot up and two men killed. Then members of its Londonderry unit machine-gunned the lounge bar of the Rising Sun bar in the small village of Greysteel, killing seven people (six Catholics and one Protestant). When the other victims of murders between the Shankill bomb and Greysteel were added, the death toll for one week stood at twenty-three and Northern Ireland was back in the headlines and at the centre of the British and Irish political stages. London and Dublin talked of the desperate need for political progress. Hume talked grandly of being able to deliver 'peace in a week' if John Major would just accept the scheme he had worked out with Sinn Fein. Molyneaux was sceptical. Paisley was scathing: 'They're saying "You can have peace if you surrender within a week."'[19] And, as was becoming increasingly common, an editorial in the usually staid *Ulster News Letter* agreed with his analysis.

Turning Stomachs

In early November newspapers started to report rumours of contacts between the government and the IRA. These were met with outright denials that went so far as to attack the judgement of the DUP politicians who made them. A Northern Ireland Office spokesman reacted to one such claim from Nigel Dodds by saying:

The Secretary of State has said on many occasions that there will be no talking to the IRA or any other violent group of people unless or until they have said that violence is at an end and shown that they mean it.

That remains the position. It's worth noting that this allegation lacks the essential details by which the truthfulness of any new story is judged—who, where, when for a start. As such it belongs more purely in the fantasy world of spy thrillers than in real life.[20]

In the immediate aftermath of the fish-shop bomb and the Greysteel murders, Major explicitly ruled out talks with the IRA and memorably said that talking with Sinn Fein 'would make my stomach turn'. But on 15 November Adams claimed that there had been extensive and protracted contacts between Sinn Fein and the government, contacts that had been broken off in order to placate unionist politicians. This was heavily denied by Downing Street and by Sir Patrick Mayhew, who said on BBC Radio's *Today* programme: 'Nobody has been authorized to talk or to negotiate on behalf of the British government with Sinn Fein. We have always made it clear that there will be no talking or negotiating with Sinn Fein or any other organization that justified violence.'[21] Two days later, leading Sinn Fein member Martin McGuinness confirmed that he had been in direct contact and dialogue with the British government. Again the Northern Ireland Office and Downing Street denied the claims.

The story was given a new twist when the DUP claimed that the increased frequency of troops patrolling in berets rather than helmets was proof that there were negotiations between the British government and the IRA. While Downing Street, the Northern Ireland Office, and the Foreign Office all denied that there were contacts with the republican movement, Paisley said: 'The change from helmets to berets is only the tip of the iceberg. A complete capitulation is in the offing in order to secure a manipulated cease-fire to aid the sell-out to Dublin.'[22] Then, two days later and for a very short time, Paisley seemed reassured by the Prime Minister. After an hour-long meeting between Major and the three DUP Members of Parliament, Paisley recounted to the press that Major had robustly rejected a scheme leaked from Dublin that suggested all-Ireland boards with executive powers. In what sounded like a feeble attempt to match Paisley's style, Major supposedly said that, had any such scheme been presented to him, he would have 'kicked it over the house tops'.

Paisleyite happiness with the Prime Minister was short-lived. After further details of contacts between the government and the IRA were published in the *Observer*, the contacts were admitted and a full statement was made to the House of Commons. To accompany this, Mayhew presented what purported to be summaries of the messages that had been exchanged. According to Sir Patrick, the chronology of contacts was as follows.

At the end of February this year, a message was received from the IRA leadership. It said: The conflict is over but we need your advice on how to bring it to a close. We wish to have an unannounced cease-fire in order to hold dialogue leading to peace. We cannot announce such a move as it will lead to confusion for the volunteers because the press will misinterpret it as surrender. We cannot meet the Secretary of State's public renunciation of violence, but it would be given privately as long as we were sure that we were not being tricked. The message came from Martin McGuinness.[23]

On 22 March a representative of the government met IRA leaders and handed over a document prepared by Mayhew. There were then a further twenty exchanges before contact was broken off in November.

There was a mixed response to the House of Commons statement. Generally, the British press welcomed the realism shown by the contacts and readily forgave the denials. Conservative MPs were reassured that the substance of the government's messages was consistent with the publicly stated policy that republicans could join talks only if they renounced violence. Predictably, Ulster unionists were less happy and Paisley was least happy of all. Perhaps infuriated by the way in which the Northern Ireland Office had ridiculed as 'fantasy' his party's claims that such talks were going on, Paisley persisted in calling Mayhew a liar and was ejected from the Commons.

More disturbing for unionists was the announcement from McGuinness that the British government and the IRA had been in contact throughout the 1980s. During the hunger-strikes there had been meetings sanctioned by Thatcher. In April 1991 a British official told McGuinness that the loyalist paramilitaries were about to announce a cease-fire for the inter-party talks. Between June and Christmas the same year there had been a number of meetings at which British officials had briefed Sinn Fein on British policy.

Also ominous was the IRA's denial of the accuracy of the government's account of how the meetings began. McGuinness said: 'Patrick Mayhew read a text which he claims to be a communication sent by me to the British government in late February. I totally refute his claim. The text he read is a counterfeit. No such communication was ever sent. It is a lie, yet another lie which has emanated from Patrick Mayhew and John Major in recent times.'[24] Mayhew then admitted that there had been some typing errors in the production of the various documents for the Commons but insisted that the basic tenor of the communication was accurately reported.

McGuinness's denial is central to the interpretation of the significance of the talks. Since John Hume's talks with Adams, the interpretation of signs has come down to a rather simple question. Is the IRA actually ready to give up the armed struggle? I will return to that shortly.

The Downing Street Declaration

Although the government in Dublin had initially been hostile to the Hume–Adams talks and leaked its disapproval widely to the press, Deputy Prime Minister Dick Spring took up the running by announcing 'six principles' which should govern future progress. In contrast to his suggestion the previous year of imposing joint authority on Northern Ireland, his principles now included the recognition that unionists had the freedom to withhold their consent from change unless they could be persuaded by democratic means.[25]

Major and Reynolds announced that they would now give their full attention to Northern Ireland. Meetings were planned. Great progress was hinted at and then ominous hints of difficulties were dropped. Summits were announced and then scaled down to working meetings. Reynolds let it be known that he was unhappy about London's secret talks with the IRA. London let it be known that it was unhappy about Reynolds's desire for simultaneous referenda on the future of Northern Ireland north and south of the border. On 5 December *Scotland on Sunday* headed its story 'Christmas peace hopes fade'; the *Observer* went for 'Dangerous illusion at the heart of the Irish summit'. Two days later, the *Independent* announced: 'Ulster declaration stalled by impasse over aspirations.'[26]

And then, with that flourish much loved by politicians in need of a good press, Major and Reynolds announced their joint Downing Street declaration. The document was difficult to interpret, being, as one British commentator put it, 'the worst-written document ever to have a claim on posterity's attention'.[27] It was certainly easy to believe, as one source reported, that eighteen drafts passed back and forth between the two governments before a final version was agreed.

The introduction contained a number of phrases pleasing to nationalists: 'Both [governments] recognise that the ending of divisions can only come about through the agreement and co-operation of the people, North and South, representing both traditions in Ireland,' and 'They therefore make a solemn commitment to promote co-operation at all levels on the basis of the fundamental principles, undertakings, obligations under international agreements, to which they have jointly committed themselves.' This latter seems clearly to reaffirm the Anglo-Irish accord processes. But there was also something for unionists in the mention of 'the guarantees which each government has given and now reaffirms, including Northern Ireland's statutory constitutional guarantee'. Considering how opposed Major had been to closer European integration, it is ironic that he accepted what was clearly an SDLP reference to the hope that 'the development of Europe will, of itself, require new approaches to serve interests common to both parts of the island of Ireland'.

For unionists, the crucial text came at the start of the 'singular-voice' sections, when paragraph 4 said: 'The Prime Minister, on behalf of the British government, reaffirms that they will uphold the democratic wish of the greater number of the people of Northern Ireland on the issue of whether they prefer to support the Union or a sovereign united Ireland.' But such comfort as could be derived from that was rather snatched away by the next sentence, which said that the British government had 'no selfish strategic or economic interest in Northern Ireland. Their primary interest is to see peace, stability and reconciliation established by agreement among all the people who inhabit the island, and they will work together with the Irish government to achieve such an agreement, which will embrace the totality of relationships.' As a number of people were to note, this was a very long way from Thatcher's assertion that Northern Ireland was as British as Finchley, and prompted Conservative MP Nicholas Budgen to ask if the Prime Minister would now confirm that the government had 'a strategic or economic interest in Wolverhampton'. Further, that section had a number of SDLP phrases in it, in particular the reference to the 'totality of relationships', which had been used by Hume to deny that there could be any settlement in Northern Ireland that did not have an executive role for Dublin.

Paragraph 5, the Dublin voice, also sought to have something for nationalists and unionists. Though it made the point in a back-handed manner that reminded people that Britain caused the Troubles by partitioning the island in 1920, the Reynolds part went further than any previous statement in accepting that unionists could not be coerced into a united Ireland when it said:

The Taoiseach ... considers that the lessons of Irish history, and especially of Northern Ireland, show that stability and well-being will not be found under any political system which is refused allegiance or rejected on grounds of identity by a significant minority of those governed by it.

For this reason, it would be wrong to attempt to impose a united Ireland, in the absence of the freely given consent of a majority of the people of Northern Ireland.[28]

In a number of different ways, the same point was made repeatedly. For example, the declaration said: 'Both governments accept that Irish unity would be achieved only by those who favour this outcome persuading those who do not, peacefully and without coercion or violence.' Dublin also promised that, in the context of an overall settlement, the constitution of the Irish Republic would be changed.

But what, apart from the usual bromides, was actually being suggested? The only parts that might be called plans were extremely vague. The two governments promised to seek 'along with the Northern Ireland constitutional parties through a process of political dialogue, to create institutions and structures which, while respecting the diversity of the people of Ireland, would enable them to work together in all areas of common interest'.

There was the commitment from the Irish government to

make their own arrangements within their jurisdiction to enable democratic parties to consult together and share in dialogue about the political future. The Taoiseach's intention is that these arrangements could include the establishment . . . of a Forum for Peace and Reconciliation to make recommendations on ways in which agreement and trust between both traditions in Ireland can be promoted and established.

That unionists would immediately refuse to be involved in any such discussions with a 'foreign power' was inevitable.

But the most significant part of the declaration was that section which sought to build on the promise implicit in the still secret Hume–Adams document and in the exchange of messages with the IRA (especially in the crucial one which McGuinness claimed was a fabrication!). The declaration promised that former terrorists would 'be free to participate fully in democratic politics and to join in dialogue in due course between the governments and the political parties on the way ahead'. If the IRA declared an end to its campaign of violence, after a brief period to test that commitment Sinn Fein would be allowed to join in reconvened talks about the future.

Almost more interesting than the declaration itself were two attendant details, one of which preceded the declaration and one which followed it. In a manner very similar to the British contacts with the IRA, Dublin had for some months been in communication with the loyalist paramilitaries. To increase the chances of the declaration receiving at least a quiet reception (an enthusiastic welcome was obviously out of the question), Reynolds had provided the UVF with a copy of the Downing

Street text the day before it was released and it in turn had passed a copy to the UDA and the Red Hand Commando.

Also keen to placate unionist feelings, Major appended to the declaration a list of things that the unionists should note he had not promised. The list, attached to the copy of the declaration distributed by the Northern Ireland Information Service, was as follows:

The joint Declaration does not:

- assert the value of achieving a united Ireland nor assert the legitimacy of a united Ireland in the absence of majority consent
- commit the British government to join the ranks of the persuaders for a united Ireland
- set any timescale for a united Ireland to come about nor indicate that this is even probable
- commit the people of Northern Ireland to joining a united Ireland against their democratic wishes
- establish arrangements for the exercise of joint authority between the British and Irish governments over Northern Ireland
- derogate in any way from UK sovereignty over Northern Ireland, nor diminish the constitutional guarantee
- contain any reference or implicit commitment to the withdrawal of British troops from Northern Ireland
- give Sinn Fein any immediate place at the Talks table
- sideline the valuable round of meetings with the Northern Ireland parties being undertaken by Michael Ancram. On the contrary, it speaks of transforming the prospects for building on the progress already made.[29]

The Aftermath

Not surprisingly, given that the declaration followed Hume's own logic in presenting as a solution what was clearly a paradox (both the people of Ireland, that is a nationalist majority, and the people of Northern Ireland, that is a unionist majority, have a right to self-determination), he was warmly supportive and promised to continue his discussions with Adams to persuade him to join in the peace process.

There was much speculation about just exactly what would follow for the IRA. Reynolds began to talk about amnesties for prisoners. Republican prisoners in the Maze were quick to see that they were being used as a source of leverage on Northern minority opinion, with the promise of their release designed to put pressure on them and their families to press the IRA to accept a settlement. Reynolds and Major went out of their way to couple this excellent opportunity for the IRA with a very clear threat that there would be a security crackdown if the chance of peace was rejected. Adams felt he could wring more concessions out of the British and called for direct negotiations with the British and Irish governments. They rejected that call, but who would believe them?[30]

Even if one did not read the declaration, it is clear from the efforts that Reynolds and Major put into selling it to the loyalist paramilitaries and to the Ulster unionists that the declaration was not something they would like. An early opinion poll confirmed that in Northern Ireland the declaration was being seen as favouring the nationalists. Of those polled, 56 per cent backed it but that single figure disguised a considerable difference between nationalists and unionists. Eighty-seven per cent of nationalists and only 43 per cent of unionists were in favour. Fifty-two per cent of people thought it had strengthened the nationalist position but only 7 per cent thought it had weakened it.[31]

In line with the pattern of responses to initiatives since the Anglo-Irish accord, the UUP gave the declaration a very guarded and cautious welcome, if we can describe as a welcome Molyneaux pressing Major to reaffirm that the future of Northern Ireland would be decided by the people of Northern Ireland and his statement that unionists had nothing to fear from the document. He did not add, but others did, that they also had nothing to gain from it. It was left to the DUP to do the shouting. Peter Robinson declared that 'The DUP is not suckered by Dublin humbug and hogwash. Reconciliation is on their lips but not in their hearts.'[32] Paisley again stressed the pointlessness of appeasement of the IRA. Speaking to Major in the House, he said:

As a public representative, I find it very offensive to be told that in three months' time, if the IRA cease from their violence, without any conditions of handing over their weapons or their bomb-making materials, that they will be invited as constitutional politicians to sit down. Your constituents have not been butchered or murdered. Maybe you would like to sit down with the godfathers of the people who would do it.[33]

The DUP had allies in an unusual quarter. A number of Dublin liberals, most particularly Conor Cruise O'Brien, felt that the declaration, while quite unlikely to do enough to persuade the IRA to end its campaign of violence, went a long way to reconstruct the sense of the Northern Ireland problem, and where its solution lay, in a nationalist direction.[34] Perhaps surprisingly, given the unsympathetic press reception for Paisley's outburst in the House, a number of British commentators also saw the declaration as representing a serious shift in government policy. Andrew Rawnsley in the *Observer* commented that 'The Conservatives have, as near as makes no difference, embraced Labour's policy of unification by consent. So the IRA has "won".'[35] As a leader put it in the *Independent*:

Ulster Protestants see themselves as British rather than Irish, and though for many years they have suspected the British across the water do not return this description, they still do not expect British prime ministers to fall in with the ideology of republicanism and treat their part of the United Kingdom as a colony. When the British government declared that it has 'no selfish strategic or economic interest' in Northern Ireland it might have been speaking of a disaffected territory in the Indian Ocean rather than the neat hedgerows of County Down and the British municipal splendour of Belfast City Hall'.[36]

I have already suggested that British thinking about Northern Ireland could be encapsulated in the proposition of cultivating the 'liberal' centre. Over the years the government has been keen to keep Molyneaux briefed (and his position as a Privy Counsellor would mean that he was kept informed of sensitive issues) and has wanted to rid itself of Ian Paisley. John Major's reliance on UUP votes to pass the Maastricht treaty and to maintain his government with its slender majority has merely strengthened what was already the government's tendency. In particular, the integrationist wing of the UUP was comforted by the promise of a Select Committee to scrutinize Northern Ireland legislation. Although of little practical value, it would have important symbolism by bringing Northern Ireland into line with Scotland in the treatment of its specific legislation.

Paisley and the DUP were vehemently dismissive of the declaration, describing it bluntly as 'the Anglo-Irish accord Mark 2'. The UDA was initially keen to distance itself from Paisley's knee-jerk rejection. One source quoted in the *Irish News* said: 'While a lot of people agree with what Paisley is saying, we will not be joining him. He has been down this road so many times before.'[37] The Combined Loyalist Military Command (CLMC) put out the following statement:

We are in receipt of the recent joint declaration issued by the British and Irish governments, the contents of which are being studied and analysed at this moment in time in conjunction with the principles issued by the CLMC on 10th December 1993.

A comprehensive response will be made in due course after clarification on certain issues has been sought and received. In the interim period and in the absence of any response from the Provisional murder gangs, the CLMC will pursue its stated policy in relation to IRA violence.

In order to allay immediate loyalist fears and to maximise Unionist unity the CLMC calls for a forum to be instituted to encompass all the loyalist and unionist political parties in Ulster.[38]

Contained in the statement was some clever drafting. The point about clarification was copied from the Sinn Fein response and the phrase 'Provisional murder gangs' was a direct copy of the phrase Sinn Fein normally uses to refer to the UVF and UDA. The final point about a unionist forum was also a neat copy of Albert Reynolds's plan for a consultative forum independent of the British government's continuing talks with constitutional parties in Northern Ireland. The statement was actually a compromise. There were people in the UVF who wanted a full cease-fire to call the IRA's bluff and intensify pressure on the republican movement. However, the UDA leaders were not in favour and were initially planning a more robust rejection of the joint declaration. It is important to note, however, that, when some UDA men dubbed the UVF 'the Peace People', they were engaging in insults rather than analysis. As has been the case for a number of years, the UVF was more overtly welcoming of prospects of peace but at the same time was also arming for war. On 24 November, just two weeks before the Downing Street declaration, a cargo of 300 assault rifles and two tons of explosives bought from Poland was intercepted at Teesport on its way to the UVF.

PROSPECTS FOR PEACE?

As of the time of writing—New Year's Day 1994—it is still too early to be sure of the IRA's response to the declaration, but the signs are not good. Since the end of its traditional Christmas truce, the IRA has murdered two soldiers and bombed a large number of shops in Belfast, and Martin McGuinness has reaffirmed the IRA's view that nothing short of a British declaration of intention to leave Northern Ireland will suffice.[39]

While waiting to see which way the republican movement goes, it is possible to inspect the auguries. If we take them at face value, the statements and actions of John Hume and the British and Dublin governments all suppose that the IRA is tired and wishes to end its campaign. On the one hand, we have to respect their judgements and suppose that the security forces are well briefed by their spies within the Provisional IRA. On the other hand, it is not easy to see why the IRA should now be thinking of throwing in the towel. One sensible reading of the last twenty-five years is that the IRA's terror campaign has gone rather well. The Stormont state has been destroyed. The nationalist SDLP has been put in the position of having a veto on future developments. The Anglo-Irish accord has given a formal position of influence to the Dublin government. Sinn Fein has established itself as the voice of a significant section of the nationalists in the North.

But, even if republicans took a pessimistic view and instead counted the costs of their terror on the economic well-being of their communities or contemplated their own fatalities, in so far as they could see these as reasons for stopping, they would also see them as reasons for demanding a high price for peace. They will not easily forget their martyrs: the eight men shot dead in an ambush at Loughgall, the two men and a women shot dead in Gibraltar, the ten dead hunger-strikers. And all those years served in prison.

Putting together those two sets of observations leads very many observers to be sceptical about the chances of the IRA going home and leaving Sinn Fein to behave like a conventional political party. Remember that Sinn Fein gets only some 10 per cent of the vote in Northern Ireland. The best it is being offered is an opportunity to join the Mayhew talks. Even assuming that one or both of the unionist parties do not boycott such talks, we are merely back to the position of the end of the strand-1 talks in 1992. The unionist parties with the support of the British government will sign up for a complex system of power-sharing (although no one will call it that), and the SDLP, now presumably accompanied by Sinn Fein, will reject anything that does not have a formal executive Dublin role. Strand-2 talks will get nowhere at all and the whole business will collapse. At that point the IRA will conclude that it has achieved nothing and will be tempted to go back to terror. But if there has been any period of peace—even a few months—there may be considerable opposition in working-class Catholic areas to going back to war. If we can reason along those lines, then so can the IRA, and such reasoning is unlikely to tempt them to lose their present momentum.

It may well be that the British and Dublin governments have come to the same conclusion and see the declaration, not as a solution to the problem, but as a way of isolating the IRA so that some vigorous security response (such as the return of internment but this time on both sides of the border) will be acceptable and effective. Alternatively, and this is where the real fears of loyalists lie, it may be that the IRA has been promised something else. While the two governments are publicly basing their process on the belief that the IRA is tired and ready to give up, it may be that it is the British government which is tired and ready to give up. Given that it spent so long denying that it was in contact with the IRA before it admitted such contacts, the government denying that there is a second secret deal on the table for the IRA will not be terribly persuasive.

4. THE LOYALIST AGENDA

So that we can see clearly where the loyalists are now and where they might go politically, I will briefly review the history of the political positions of the loyalist paramilitaries and of the evangelicals, and then try to explain what it is they want, are prepared to accept, or will oppose with degrees of violence.

THE UVF

Initially the UVF was simply an ultra-unionist organization, but during the early years of his imprisonment Gusty Spence became ever more distanced from traditional unionism. He became critical of the UUP and of the Stormont regime, partly because it was not willing to defend itself and partly because he felt that he and his men had been 'used'. Nineteen years later, reflecting on the climate in 1966, he said: 'Tension and apprehension were running high. Then one month before the election an IRA plot to wipe out the entire cabinet in Stormont was uncovered. Somehow the Unionists always seemed to discover one before elections.'[1] He happily adopted the nationalist description of the UUP's tenure as 'fifty years of misrule' and became almost socialist in his general views. That loyalists had enjoyed élite support for their culture was no longer sufficient consolation for the poverty of many working-class Protestant areas. Though highly critical of the republican movement, he did accept that the Catholics in Northern Ireland had to be given some say in running the place and in the 1980s was even willing to see Sinn Fein involved in talks: 'If people are democratically and constitutionally elected then you have to take account of them, that is if you are a democrat. Sooner or later someone will have to talk to them.'[2] Yet, for all that, he remained a loyalist, committed to the union with Great Britain and to the history and traditions of the Protestant people of Ulster.

Spence had considerable influence with a small number of UVF men, but in the 1970s the majority were little moved by his democratic socialism or his acceptance of Catholics in the Northern Ireland state. Sarah Nelson's *Ulster's Uncertain Defenders*, though excellent in many respects, makes the mistake of giving more attention to the political thinking of some UVF leaders than the UVF gave.[3] Men joined the UVF because they wanted to defend the state, not because they wanted politics lessons. Anyway, in the Long Kesh compounds, Spence was isolated from the organization, and, in contrast to the situation in the republican movement, the loyalist prisoners did not become a major source of political ideas and inspiration for the organizations outside. Many UVF leaders were openly scornful of Spence's moderation. The loathing was mutual; Spence thought them dwarfs.

In the summer of 1973 some UVF men were active in promoting the short-lived Ulster Loyalist Front, a Shankill Road group that had two elected councillors, and which was primarily concerned with the rights of loyalist prisoners: it wanted the return of jury trials and the release of all internees. Prisoners were also a major concern of the next initiative: the Volunteer Political Party (VPP), which was launched in the aftermath of the successful 1974 UWC strike. The VPP was a curious animal. It was brought into being by men who thought the UVF should be doing something positive to complement its terrorism. It had a membership—all Volunteers were enrolled—but, as the *Combat* editorial announcing the party frankly admitted, it had no policy. 'Another requirement is the formulation of a policy document which embraces all shades of opinion within the organization. In order to achieve this as quickly as possible we ask all interested personnel to submit to the Political Executive their proposals.'[4] The VPP fielded one candidate, Ken Gibson, in the Westminster elections of October 1974, he got only 14 per cent of the unionist vote in West Belfast. The VPP dissolved itself.

Alderman Hughie Smyth, one of the founders of the United Loyalist Front and a long-serving councillor for an area of Belfast where the UVF is strong, formed the Independent Unionist group (which later became the Progressive Unionist Party (PUP)) as a vehicle for the kinds of ideas that Spence had been promoting. For a short time after his release from prison, Spence worked for the PUP. Though Smyth retains his following on the Shankill and the party has had a number of councillors elected, it has failed to dent the domination of the UUP and DUP. Even in the city council ward which includes the Shankill, Pentecostal pastor and DUP councillor Eric Smyth got more first-preference votes than Smyth (in 1993 2,300 to 1,600).

Except indirectly through sharing common views with the PUP, the UVF has no vehicle other than the magazine *Combat* and the occasional brigade-staff statement for political expression. Its leaders accept that it cannot be a powerful independent political force; such a role must be left to the politicians. However, the more thoughtful members of brigade staff, thinking along Spence lines, have sometimes used their position to chivvy their political representatives, as they did in the run-up to the Brooke talks. One of the architects of the cease-fire told me:

The cease-fire was genuine. The UVF did not want to give unionist politicians any excuse to be intransigent. We wanted a reasonable accommodation and we wanted to force them to work and do their job. But we also wanted them to know that we cannot accept Dublin rule. Bills of Rights, shared responsibility for Catholics and Protestants, whatever; they could have all that. But not Dublin rule.

Through the Combined Loyalist Military Command, the UVF leaders have continued to try to keep a united front with the UDA.

THE UDA AND NEGOTIATED INDEPENDENCE

That the UDA recruited from a wider base than the UVF and permitted a category of members who were not involved in 'military' activities meant that it was always more likely to produce political innovation, and that proved to be the case. Much of the thinking came from Glen Barr and the others involved in the 1974 strike. Once they had won, the paramilitary leaders held a three-day conference to discuss the way forward. Barr failed to persuade the others to support his idea of negotiated independence and the UVF was particularly opposed.

Barr left the UDA in 1975 when Bill Craig's Vanguard Party (of which Barr was an elected representative) split. In the constitutional convention that followed the collapse of the Executive, Bill Craig promoted the notion of a 'voluntary coalition' with the SDLP. He was convinced that the convention was the last chance to retain some sort of devolved government in the province. Institutional power-sharing was not a possibility, but Craig believed that the various emergency coalitions that the British government had adopted in such times of national crisis as the Second World War offered a model. Formally the system of government would be the conventional one of rule by the largest party, but, if the unionists won, they would invite SDLP leaders to hold office on the basis of agreement with the policy of the governing party on major issues.

Voluntary coalition would not have worked—it is hard to imagine the SDLP being able to agree with any security policy which tried to control republican terror—but Barr believed it was worth a chance. The anti-power-sharing Ulster Unionists, the Democratic Unionists, and a large number of Vanguard activists rejected voluntary coalition—that was to be expected—but Barr hoped the UDA would back the idea. Sammy Smyth, one of the other thinkers in the UDA, was extremely critical and Andy Tyrie was opposed. After the UDA tried to muzzle him, Barr withdrew.

He was invited back in 1977 when the UDA had foolishly allowed itself to be drawn into a second general strike, which, for a number of reasons, was a failure. Tyrie wanted Barr to help run the strike. Barr was sure the strike would fail and only came back to help get the UDA off the hook. With Harry Chicken, Bill Snoddy, and Tommy Lyttle, he formed the New Ulster Political Research Group (NUPRG) to produce a coherent political direction for the UDA.

Although Barr and Chicken already knew what they wanted, almost a year of weekly meetings was spent hammering out the details, and almost as much effort was put into selling the proposals to the rank-and-file of the UDA. They also sold the need for restraint in killing: in 1975 and 1976 there had been 114 and 113 loyalist murders; in 1977 and 1978 the numbers were twenty-five and eight. At the end of the process of consultation, they could claim to have a full mandate from the UDA to press the case for negotiated independence. Barr made it sound very obvious:

We need to create a system of government, an identity and a nationality to which both sections of the community can aspire. We must look for the common denominator. The only common denominator that the Ulster people have, whether they be Catholic or Protestant, is that they are Ulstermen. And that is the basis from which we should build the new life for the Ulster people, a new identity for them. Awaken them to their own identity. That they are different. That they're not second-class Englishmen but first-class Ulstermen. And that's where my loyalty is.[5]

The proposed constitution was modelled on that of the United States. There would be a directly elected president, who would choose an executive, preferably of academic and professional people rather than politicians. The executive would answer to committees drawn from an elected legislature. There would be a detailed bill of rights and a judiciary responsible for safeguarding civil liberties.

In November 1978 the policy was published as *Beyond the Religious Divide* and immediately attracted favourable responses from people across the political spectrum. An early supporter was Paddy Devlin, one of the SDLP leaders closest to the working-class trade-unionist background of Barr and Chicken. There followed a year of speaking engagements. The NUPRG members travelled to the United States and were well received by a number of US politicians. They addressed meetings in Dublin, Holland, and England as well as innumerable gatherings in Northern Ireland. But, although Barr and Chicken won the admiration of many disinterested commentators, they failed to convert any of the major parties to the idea of negotiated independence. When all was said and done, unionists wanted either full integration with Britain or a return to Stormont, and nationalists wanted either a united Ireland or (as a temporary measure) institutionally guaranteed power-sharing in a devolved government.

The NUPRG had not only to contend with external critics; there were also rumblings within the UDA. One brigadier objected to giving brigade funds to support the political work: 'I couldn't see the point. It was never going to do nothing.' Others resented the prominence of Barr and Chicken. A few senior figures were critical of their policy. One such critic was John McMichael. McMichael rose through the ranks of the Lisburn Defence Association to become brigadier of South Belfast. Although no intellectual, he was more articulate than many UDA commanders. He became slightly involved in Harry Chicken's Ulster Community Action Group and was then secretary to the NUPRG. He made little contribution to the discussions and appears to have been there as something of a 'minder'. Unlike the others, he was active on the military side of the organization and was responsible for planning and approving many of the UFF's assassinations.

Despite McMichael's apparent agreement with the NUPRG's positions, he privately caused dissension by, as one man put it, 'poisoning Andy's mind about us'. Being a close friend of Tyrie, he was able to voice his suspicions of the UDA's political direction and he was especially critical of the Northern Ireland Negotiated Independence Association, a committee formed to connect the NUPRG to other small groups committed to that direction. He is widely suspected of alienating Tyrie's affections with the whispered observation that there were 'too many Taigs' involved, and he did his best to kill any possibility of cross-divide support by trying to have it named the *Ulster* Negotiated Independence Association.

Without any dramatic or very public split, Barr and Chicken withdrew from the UDA, with Barr diplomatically claiming ill health. John McMichael became the UDA's chief political spokesman. The change in direction became clear in 1981 with the formation of the Ulster Loyalist Democratic Party (ULDP). As its name—not only *Ulster* but also *Loyalist*—made clear, the new party represented a step back from the NUPRG position. In response to criticisms that the UDA was a 'Prod Sinn Fein', the ULDP offered a more limited independence within the United Kingdom. As McMichael explained it: 'We found that although people feel anti-Westminster and anti-English they still have a great affection for the monarchy. So it would be independence within the EEC and the Commonwealth, which we think would be acceptable to many Roman Catholics.'[6]

The next phase in the UDA's politics followed the shock to the loyalist system of the Anglo-Irish accord. Peter Robinson and other DUP leaders helped form the Ulster Clubs as a new vehicle to co-ordinate grass-roots protest. McMichael, who was much influenced by Robinson and saw the Clubs as a way of attracting a 'better class' of person to the UDA, was given a place on the steering committee. Against a background of political protest, public disorder, and an increase in sectarian assassination, the UDA in January 1987 published *Common Sense*, which borrowed extensively from *Beyond the Religious Divide* but kept Northern Ireland firmly within the United Kingdom. There would be no return to majority rule but neither would there be the anathema of institutionalized power-sharing. Instead there would be 'proportionality' at every stage of government. Positions would be allocated on the basis of proportion of votes gained. The final paragraphs were stirring:

The pragmatic alternative to co-determination is to fight a bloody civil war and let the victor dictate the rules by which we will live.

What we propose will probably be described by some as idealistic, ambitious, fraught with difficulties and even dangerous to attempt but then so has anything that was ever worth doing. The most dangerous thing to do, and unfortunately the most politically popular, would be to do NOTHING.

As had been the case with *Beyond*, the proposals were hailed in editorials as 'brave', described by a Roman Catholic cardinal as 'fresh and constructive', accepted by the SDLP as a basis for negotiation, and condemned by unionist politicians as power-sharing. The impact of *Common Sense* was the same as that of *Beyond the Religious Divide*: very little. However much some people were impressed that a paramilitary organization could produce a reasoned and imaginative policy document, the major parties ignored it and there was no pressure from the public for them to do otherwise. With its name changed to the Ulster Democratic Party (UDP) and led by McMichael's son Gary, the party continues, but the extent of its influence on the 'operators' within the UDA is probably slight. Especially since the UDA was banned, the UDP insists that, unlike Sinn Fein for the IRA, it is not a paramilitary front. In at least one important sense it is not: it does not have the influence on the UDA that Sinn Fein has on the IRA.

With the retirement of Andy Tyrie, the UDA lost the leader who had done most to promote first Barr and then McMichael. The banning of the organization in 1992 reduced its pretensions and made it much more like the UVF—primarily a terrorist organization which accepts the division of labour: we do violence, politicians do politics. However, the recognition that they are not going to be powerful political players does not mean that the UDA and UVF contribute nothing to the political debates. Even when the two organizations recognize that their specific policies are of little account, they none the less intend to retain the ability to chivvy their political leaders and to present a powerful veto on developments which they find unacceptable. The limits of what can be accepted are, in the context of remaining unionist, quite generous. Under the name of the Ulster Loyalist Central Co-ordinating Committee, the UDA and UVF in 1992 issued a joint statement which repeated the common ground. They offered a written constitution and a bill of rights, proportional representation in all elections, and the general theme that, however it was constructed, executive power and responsibility should be based on proportionality or some form of voluntary coalition. That is, most things internal will be fine.

The definition of the unacceptable was that which would anyway have been shared by every unionist politician: 'Over the years the loyalist working class has stood firm against any unwanted interference by the government of the Republic of Ireland in the internal affairs of Northern Ireland.'[7] And it would continue to do so.

While unionist politicians were vocal in their condemnation of John Hume for his hard-line nationalism in the constitutional talks and for his negotiations with the political representatives of the IRA, the UDA announced that it now saw no obvious difference between armed republicans and constitutional nationalists. Both were the enemies of Ulster; both were part of a 'pan-nationalist front'. This statement was accompanied in August and September 1993 by a series of bomb attacks on SDLP politicians. Fortunately no one was injured and, although two devices were placed under cars and may well have been intended to maim or to kill, others were placed in gardens of houses, which rather suggests that the primary purposes were to intimidate and to warn. Threats were also made against the Gaelic Athletic Association (GAA), which is committed to the goal of a united Catholic Gaelic Ireland and which permits members of the IRA but not members of the RUC to join.[8] The ridiculous was not entirely absent from this loyalist attempt to redefine the enemy. The very small and recently not very significant Red Hand Commando justified an attack on a particular Belfast pub by saying that it had been targeted for hosting Irish traditional music evenings! Two days later, and once all the jokes had been made, the Red Hand rather sheepishly announced that it was withdrawing its threat to promoters of fiddle and whistle music.

At the same time there were rumblings of experiments with home-made explosives. Incendiary devices were placed in Dublin shops. The RUC warned that it was not a question of *if* the UFF would bomb Dublin but *when* it would do it.

For all that the discovery of a pan-nationalist front was announced as a revelation, loyalist terrorists had often attacked constitutional nationalists and such Irish institutions as the GAA in the early part of the Troubles. Austin Currie, Nationalist MP at Stormont and founder member of the SDLP, was attacked by loyalists, as were his wife and family. SDLP Senator Paddy Wilson was murdered by the UFF in 1972. In 1973 and 1974 there were a number of attacks on the premises of the Gaelic Athletic Association and leading GAA men were murdered. But after 1976, though the 'yoblettes' and juvenile delinquents sometimes torched a GAA club, Catholic chapel or school, or Hibernian hall, the serious operators confined themselves to high-profile targets who were close to the republican movement (members of the National H-Block Committee, for example) or to very ordinary Catholics killed as retaliatory 'frighteners'. To put it another way, the notion of a 'legitimate target' was in theory defined fairly narrowly, and the *modus operandi* was to attack such targets or people who could, however implausibly, be claimed as legitimate targets. Hence attacks on individuals rather than big bombs in pubs. Hence famous republicans or taxi-drivers who could be claimed as IRA operators or intelligence officers.

In that sense the attacks on SDLP politicians, even if they were just threats rather than serious attempts to kill or to injure, did represent a change—not an innovation but a return to the violence of the early 1970s. They were also part of the general pattern of the last two years of the UDA being much more likely than the UVF to respond to changes 'militarily'. In Chapter 3 I mentioned the arguments between the two organizations about how they should react to the Shankill Road bomb. In the 1970s the UDA Inner Council was more likely than the UVF brigade staff to be thinking politically and much more likely to try to lead a united paramilitary response; in the 1990s the relationship is somewhat reversed.

ENDING LOYALIST TERROR

What is of particular importance to policy-makers is not so much what the UDA and UVF say in their policy documents as what they might actually do. That is, what is the relationship between the high-sounding rhetoric of their political proposals and the loyalist paramilitary campaign? Among the signatories to the UDA's *Common Sense* was 'Cecil Graham', which was the pseudonym of a brigadier with a considerable reputation for violence. McMichael was head of the UFF. Were McMichael, 'Cecil Graham', and others genuine in their support for the radical ideas in *Common Sense*? One has to suppose that they were serious; after all, apart from their own boredom, there was no pressure for them to produce any political initiative. They could, as the UVF rather did, simply leave the politicians to do the politics and continue doing what they did best.

Critics would describe the paramilitaries as fundamentally hypocritical—tolerant politics and intolerant murder—but it is not that simple. First, there is actually nothing illogical about having a peace plan and prosecuting a military campaign that will continue until the enemy sues for peace. That is how many wars are conducted. The more difficult question is whether, if the conditions for peace obtain (if, for example, the IRA does call an end to its terror), the loyalist paramilitaries would then switch to a whole-hearted endorsement of the policies of the UDP's *Common Sense* or the PUP's *Sharing Responsibility in Northern Ireland*? Would they suddenly emerge in unionist politics on the left of Ian Paisley, pressing for a bill of rights?

Before we can analyse the likely relationship between the politics and the violence, we need to get clear the status and significance of the politics. A major difficulty in trying to guess how loyalists will react in any future situation is that they seem less confident now of the point of having a political agenda than they did twenty years ago. However unrealistic Barr's 'negotiated-independence' plan might have been, it was a plan to which he and others were committed. One still hears of independence, but it is very much in the context of what one might have to do if someone else does this or that. A leading UDA man said:

I think it is now only a matter of time before we get dumped. I don't know what the timescale is but I am sure the British government want out. Everything they have ever done has been to undermine our position in the Union. My only hope is that when they do pull out we are still in a position to defend ourselves. That is what we are for. So, yes, I think we will end up with an independent Ulster but it is something we will have to fight for.

That was the view of the articulate terrorist. Even from someone who spends a lot of time presenting the organization's policies, there is a feeling that the best the UDA will be able to do is to react rather than to act.[9] More representative of the rank-and-file loyalist terrorist is the frustrated bewilderment of the man who told me:

Fuck it, I don't know where this thing is going. It has been going on so long now that I've stopped thinking about it ending. How can it end? We will not lose, we cannot lose. My grandfather joined the UVF to prevent a united Ireland and I joined the UDA for the same reason. Sometimes I think we are making it easier for the Taigs to win but then if we weren't smacking them they would have won years ago. But it is like trying to sail through fog. I've got no notion of what's on the cards. So what do we do? More of the same I reckon, you know?

What became clear in my interviews was that I was asking people for political preferences and projections when they were in no position to offer them, not because they were stupid, or had no politics, but because they had no faith in the mechanics of political negotiation, no faith in the honesty of most of the participants, no great confidence in their ability to predict the actions of the other players in the conflict, and little hope for a voice in future developments beyond the veto of violence. Very quickly, our talk shifted from what anyone wanted to assessments of the morale and determination of the other protagonists. What mattered much more than their own agenda (other than a grim determination to resist a united Ireland, which was resolutely expressed by every loyalist I interviewed) were their guesses about the IRA's willingness to give up, the British government's willingness to give up, and Dublin's willingness to give up.

What is clear from the 1980s (and that was without an IRA cease-fire) is that the UDA and UVF can slow down to the point of almost complete inactivity. What is required of them is not enthusiastic commitment to any political structure, though that would be good for democracy. What is required is a stand-down and that probably requires a number of conditions.

First IRA violence, if not eliminated altogether, has to be brought under such control that UDA and UVF leaders can argue that the security forces are doing a good job and will do a better one if they do not also have to fight against loyalists. The pressure for retaliation would be drastically reduced.

Revenging republican attacks is only one motive for loyalist terror. Some paramilitaries believe it right to fight against nationalism, and not just against armed-force republicanism. They would fight against a change in constitutional status no matter how democratically arrived at. In particular, they will want to fight against Dublin involvement in the North, although that will more likely take the form of attacks on Northern nationalists than bombs in Dublin; hitting the neighbour who wants the Republic to take a hand in Northern Ireland is easier than launching attacks in the South. These loyalists are the mirror image of Irish nationalists. Like the IRA, the commitment to democracy is secondary to the pursuit of ethnic interests. The loyalist case is presented as worthy of support because it is the desire of the majority in Ulster, but the primary concern is the right of their 'people'—the Protestants of Ulster—to 'self-determination'. Again, it is the UDA which has used the more militant language. For example, in November it made explicit threats to bomb Dublin: 'If they continue to get involved in Northern Ireland affairs there will be a price to pay.'[10] But there is not a lot of difference between the stated positions of the two organizations, and sources within the UDA and UVF are clear that the Irish Republic's government is seriously concerned about such threats. However, it is not obvious that there would be widespread support within the UDA and UVF or within their supporting environments for the use of terror to oppose Dublin involvement of the extent suggested in the Downing Street declaration, which is mostly a continuation of the 1985 Anglo-Irish accord. Nor, though the UDA and UVF now insist that a British withdrawal would lead to civil war, is it certain that they would start such a war. What was more often expressed was the view that, if it looked as if the Ulster Protestant people were willing to fight, then the UDA and UVF would lead that fight. I interpret this reticence as being in part just caution: there is no sense in putting one's head above the parapet and one's members in prison if the community is not following. But it also reflects the loosely democratic nature of the UDA and UVF. True, they are self-appointed defenders of the Protestant people and some paramilitary operators thoughtlessly exploit their own people. None the less, they need tacit support to operate extensively. Ironically, because they are closer to the working-class communities in which they live than elected politicians (one middle-class Unionist councillor for the Shankill area lives in pleasant North Down), they are subject to considerable informal control.

The desire for revenge and the need to defend one's country against pressure for constitutional change are not the only motives for Protestant paramilitary activity. Some people attack Catholics and Catholic property because they resent what they see as undue success and unfair advantage, and under any imaginable future there would be plenty of opportunity for suspecting those two things. However, my guess is that very few working-class Protestants would be drawn into expressive 'Taig-bashing'; the extent of segregation would give few opportunities for expressing frustration, and there would be very very little community support for it. Hence it would be easy to police.

However, it is important to recognize a countervailing pressure. On the loyalist as much as on the republican side, there are people whose status, power, and prestige are a result of their position within terrorist organizations. Though many operators and activists would welcome an opportunity to return to a normal life, there are some people whose aptitudes and skills would not be readily transferable and who would lose a lot with the arrival of peace. But the last sentence of the previous paragraph can be repeated here. However much some individuals may want to continue to enjoy the fruits of their reputations, a complete withdrawal of community support would allow the police readily to control such people.

Relieved of the need, or deprived of the opportunity, for terrorism, loyalist paramilitaries would probably not follow any distinct political direction. Their general responses are much more shaped by the lead given by mainstream political leaders than by that emanating from politicians closer to the UDA and UVF. That is, the general unionist and loyalist climate is more important than the specific views of the PUP or UDP, and Paisley makes a lot more weather than Hughie Smyth and Gary McMichael.

A bigger threat to future peace comes from the deep-rooted suspicions that grow with lengthy conflict in a context where one is not the master, the major player; where there actually are greater powers, or such can be imagined. I asked one UDA man: 'Let's suppose that you've won. Your campaign of terror finally persuades the IRA to renounce the armed struggle. End of hostilities. What would you do then?' The immediate answer was: 'Try to find out what the NIO [Northern Ireland Office] had promised the bastards.' What gives an air of unreality to all talk of political settlements and structures is the strong possibility that, even if they seemed to have won in their fight to keep Ulster British, loyalists would suppose their victory a hollow façade. They would suspect that, despite all appearances to the contrary, a secret deal had been done either to deliver a united Ireland at some future date or to direct social and economic policy to the advantage of Catholic areas. The conflict is now so deeply embedded that few people can imagine it not being there.

To summarize, the important question to ask about paramilitary politics is not 'are they sincere?' but what conditions are necessary for the majority of them to give up terrorism. If we want to be optimistic, we can note that the UDA and UVF have previously wound down. Though a few are addicted to the thrills, most gunmen would rather be leading dull, safe, and law-abiding lives. If we want to be pessimistic, we can note that any changes which lead to a reduction in, or an end to, republican violence will be interpreted as evidence of such major concessions to the nationalist side that some loyalists will be tempted to fight on. The extent to which they are able to do that, of course, depends on the degree of community support, and here we have to turn to the evangelicals, whose responses to any change will have greater impact on loyalist definitions of the situation than the reactions of the UDA and UVF.

THE EVANGELICALS

It has long been hoped by the British and Dublin governments that the unionist parties' leaders were unrepresentative of their electorates. Hence the structure for the Brooke–Mayhew talks, with what turned out to be unwieldy negotiating teams of ten people for each party. The idea was that, by increasing the numbers, younger and more flexible people would be brought in to the discussions and would be able to move their leaders from their well-established positions. This did not happen, and it was clear from my interviews that the positions argued by Dr Paisley and his team were supported by a wide variety of members of the evangelical loyalist rank and file. Indeed, the only dissenting voices I heard were from people expressing concern that perhaps 'the Doc' was being a bit too liberal. Some respondents wondered if age was making him less resolute in his defence of Ulster. During the 1992 talks, FP minister Ivan Foster spoke for many evangelical loyalists when he used an editorial in his periodical the *Burning Bush* to question the wisdom of unionist politicians talking to Dublin.[11] We could go further back and notice that since 1985 a number of quite senior figures have resigned from the DUP because they felt that the pact with the UUP was compromising the party's position.

Paisley's decision in September 1993 that the DUP would not be returning to constitutional talks until Dublin abandoned its claims to Northern Ireland[12] was well received, and, in his outspoken criticisms of the Hume–Adams dialogue, the talks between the British government and the IRA, and the Downing Street declaration, Paisley was speaking for and to the rural evangelicals of Ulster.

Towards the end of my research, the DUP produced *Breaking the Logjam*: its proposals for political development.[13] It argued that the SDLP's insistence on a role for Dublin made future talks between the parties pointless. The way forward lay in ascertaining the will of the people of Northern Ireland. There should be elections to an eighty-five-member assembly, which would elect a negotiating council, which would submit proposals direct to Westminster if they were passed by 60 per cent of the assembly. Paisley expected that the assembly would exclude Sinn Fein members from that council. Proposals accepted by Westminster would then be put to the people of Northern Ireland in a referendum. The ideas were immediately rejected by such nationalist voices as the *Irish News* as a return to unionist majoritarianism. Whether they were indeed just that would, of course, depend on the initial pattern of voting. It might well be that 60 per cent is high enough to ensure that SDLP agreement would be needed. But the clear impression I got from those evangelicals I asked about *Logjam* was that not even those who were DUP members thought the proposals would be widely accepted or implemented. Some candidly described them as being less a real scheme for a way forward and more a device for showing just how undemocratic the politics of Northern Ireland had become.

My discussions could be summarized as saying that most evangelicals wanted a return to the Stormont of the 1950s but accepted that it was not possible. Of the likely futures, they were willing (albeit very reluctantly) to accept something like 'power-sharing'. They were firmly opposed both to any Dublin involvement in the running of Northern Ireland and to anything that would make transition to a united Ireland easier. In that, they were at one with the paramilitaries. Where they differed was in being less militant about what they would do in the event of significant constitutional change. Some pursued a consistent democratic line and agreed that, if any genuinely representative democratic body in Northern Ireland did at some future date seek union with the Irish Republic, they would accept that decision and thereafter campaign for 'Protestant principles' in a united Ireland. Others took an Ulster nationalist position and said that in such circumstances they would be prepared to use any action (including force) to preserve a smaller Northern Ireland (Ulster east of the Bann) from a united Ireland. About half the people I interviewed fell evenly into those two camps. The rest were undecided and pragmatic in their general reply. Like the paramilitaries, how they would respond to major constitutional change would depend very much on what they took to be feasible at the time. If there was robust unionist leadership and sufficient support for opposition to change, then they would oppose it.

But, and this is where my research turned into a criticism of my original questions, the strongest impression I got from the evangelicals was that our talk about political futures was as insubstantial as foam. Like an engine revving when the clutch is not engaged, the discussion of options seemed unconnected to reality. This is not because my respondents were being insincere or because they were being unrealistic. Almost the opposite: the visions of some of them were so dismal as to cause mental paralysis. Why this should be the case becomes pretty obvious when we consider the background against which unionists are required to consider political alternatives.

There is not a lot of democratic politics going on in Northern Ireland. Stormont was closed and every alternative proposed by unionists has been rejected by the British. Councils are falling to nationalists and (despite the claims of the Derry SDLP to the contrary) very few offer a convincing example of unionists and nationalists working together. In some councils there is the absurd situation of terrorists as politicians, so neatly illustrated by the Sinn Fein councillor who complained about the injuries being caused by uneven paving stones in a shopping precinct. The IRA solved his problem by blowing up the shops. Where there are very few or no Sinn Feiners, tensions between unionists and nationalists are more politely handled, but they regularly surface, and there are always sufficient points of disagreement for each side to interpret the actions of the other as being self-serving. Councillors divide on ethnic lines when voting on community grants, the siting of council facilities, and the appointment of senior officials.

So the first difficulty of visualizing a variety of negotiated political futures and then choosing preferences is that almost no one in Northern Ireland has recent experience of even going through the motions of working democratic political institutions. Unionists may view the introduction of direct rule in 1972 as the end of democracy in Ulster, but, for all its virtues, what transpired before that can hardly be described as an exemplar of functioning democracy. Unionists and nationalists practised 'ethnic' politics in the sense of supposing that only their own people would support them. They did not compete in elections but simply worked out the ethnic carve-up. Generally, nationalists stood unopposed (except by other nationalists) in areas where Catholics were in a majority; likewise unionists in Protestant areas. The point here is not to condemn the actions of the UUP at Stormont or unionists in local councils. Contrary to the popular myths, there is a good case for arguing that in many areas of public administration (for example, in promoting agricultural efficiency and industrial innovation) the Unionist government and Unionist councils in the North did rather well. It would certainly be unfair to compare those administrations to the ethnic discriminatory regimes found in many post-colonial African states. Rather, my point is that, even for those unionists with any personal recollection of local political institutions, their operation offers few models for cross-confessional co-operation.

That the two populations have been so long locked in first the collusion of avoidance and then, from 1969, open conflict makes it very difficult for anyone to envisage 'them' as ever being on the same side as 'us'. Can any nationalist really imagine being governed by a political structure which would give executive power to Ian Paisley? Can any loyalist imagine Seamus Mallon as part of an executive that had responsibility for policing? Even if law-and-order issues were not delegated by Westminster to a new Northern Ireland body, for the SDLP to accept a settlement in Northern Ireland would mean people who have spent a quarter of a century criticizing every aspect of public administration having responsibility for large amounts of it, and that idea defies the imagination of most unionists. When all the public figures have spent so long acting as partisan spokesmen promoting the interests of their ethnic group, it is difficult to imagine them in any other role.

The length of the conflict and its bitterness have provided both an enormous amount of material for invidious stereotypes and considerable psychological pressure to hold on to such derogatory views of the other side. Bloody Sunday and La Mon House, Bloody Friday and the Shankill Butchers, Teebane and the Ormeau Road betting shop, Frizell's fish shop and

Greysteel: those incidents are combined with personal memories and with grand theories about 'them' to create just one strong notion: you cannot trust them. Exceptions will be made for the personal friend who belongs to the other side; he or she is not really like the rest of them. But, except among the very small number of saints, the antagonistic estimates of what the others are really like and what they are really up to are so strong as to make it impossible to imagine the conflict ever ending.

To conclude, the Ulster loyalists I interviewed—terrorists and evangelicals—generally had a clear and agreed constitutional vision. They would accept pretty well any internal arrangement provided it was final and not a stepping-stone to a united Ireland. They accept that there has to be some sort of weighting system to prevent the majority unionist parties ignoring nationalists. They do not want any sort of Dublin involvement, but will probably live with the present extent. But more importantly—and this is not revealed by the opinion-poll approach to research—what the two groups of loyalists shared above all was a lack of faith in the political process. For all the reasons discussed in Chapter 2, they saw themselves as beleaguered and threatened on every side. They also saw themselves firmly locked into an ethnic struggle which their opponents were determined to win, in however long a run it took. Hence Catholic nationalists were not to be trusted. Nor was the British government, which clearly placed placating Rome, the United States, Dublin, John Hume, and the IRA above defending its loyal citizens.

WHAT WILL ULSTER UNIONISTS ACCEPT?

How representative of unionist opinion are the loyalist paramilitaries and the evangelicals? Already there are many voices praising James Molyneaux's responsible attitude to the Downing Street declaration and saying that Paisley has overplayed his hand in depicting it as a sell-out to Dublin and to the IRA. In advance of the sort of electoral test that will be offered in May 1994 when leading figures from all the parties will stand in the three-member single constituency for the parliament of the European Union, it is obviously difficult accurately to assess the mood of unionists. However, there is a certain advantage in being forced to make predictions. How closely the future conforms to my assessments offers a reasonable test of my analysis.

Before offering that analysis, I would repeat an important point about research methods that I made in the Preface. By clarifying the source of my pessimism and trying to isolate what it is about my work that brings me to conclusions so much more dismal than those of many other commentators, I can make life simpler for my critics. Although the upsurge in loyalist terrorism in the early 1990s has produced an increasing number of media reports on 'Protestant alienation', I still believe that most outsiders fail to appreciate the depth of unionist unhappiness about recent political changes. In large part this is a consequence of people in Northern Ireland using public and private languages. As I have been at pains to point out at a number of points in this essay— perhaps with some exaggeration but not much—if people were as liberal and as tolerant and as accommodating and as forgiving and as unpartisan and as willing to accept the rules of liberal democracy as their public language implies, there would not have been twenty-five years of bloodshed. As I will make clear in the last chapter, what ordinary people think is not, on its own, all one needs to know, because it is in the very nature of ethnic conflict that the actions of small numbers of people can create circumstances which make people go further than they want to go. None the less, the acquiescence of large numbers of people beyond the small number of terrorists and agitators is important. I believe my understanding of what unionists *really* think is better founded than most, because loyalists and evangelicals have been prepared to talk to me as if I were one of their own. The best support I can offer for that claim is the simple fact that every previous optimistic forecast has been proved wrong.

So much for the explanation of why my prognosis is gloomier than most; back to the substance of that prognosis. The desires of the typical Ulster unionist do not seem very different from those of the two sections of unionism I have explored at length in this book. With varying amounts of nostalgia, it is accepted that the old Stormont will not return, and there is an integrationist wing of the UUP which is not altogether unhappy about that. Some sort of devolved administration would be nice. A variety of structures that prevents the majority lording it over the minority will be accepted,[14] but any simple 'divvy' of power that gives Catholics and Protestants equal say will not. It will be rejected first on the ground that it offends the theory of liberal democracy. It will be rejected secondly on the ground that it misrepresents the views of the very many Ulster Catholics who do not actually want a united Ireland in the foreseeable future. But, more pressingly, it will be rejected because, by treating all Catholics as if they were nationalists, it exaggerates the size and power of the nationalist bloc and makes it more likely that Northern Ireland will be pressed into a united Ireland.

Secondly, it seems clear to me that, though they disapprove of the violence of the terrorists and the anti-popery of the evangelicals, most unionists beyond the core of loyalism are equally resolutely opposed to any Dublin involvement in the running of Northern Ireland. The mistake commentators make is to see the difference in tone between Molyneaux and Paisley (and their lieutenants) as representing a real difference in attitudes to the major constitutional questions of the constituencies they represent. This is both to confuse style and substance and to miss the point that they operate as a 'good cop/bad cop' team! Although they will not describe their position in this way, Molyneaux supporters can distance themselves from the 'extremism' of the DUP because the DUP is there to act as a counter-weight. To make the point clear I will present it in slightly exaggerated form: were the DUP to be significantly weakened (by the death of Ian Paisley, for example), the result will not be a strengthening of the hand of the more liberal parts of the UUP but a shift to the right to compensate. In the absence of the bad cop, the good cop will become more aggressive!

One way of gauging the accuracy of that assessment is to look for the next Brian Faulkner in the UUP. Are there any creditable candidates within the Unionist Party for that role? Is there anyone likely to join Hume in running any political structure for

Northern Ireland that involves Dublin? The answer seems a very clear negative. Even someone like Robert McCartney QC, who six or seven years ago was hailed as the voice of the 'new unionism', is as resolutely opposed to the Anglo-Irish accord and its works as anyone else.[15]

But unhappiness with any future is not the same as willingness to oppose it or fight against it. There are certain sorts of political developments that do not require common consent and which cannot be prevented by boycott. The Anglo-Irish accord provided the model and it could be pressed further. London and Dublin could pursue a path which gave a gradually greater say to Dublin in the creation and appointment of unelected 'quangos' to run Northern Ireland's public administration. However, there are very many problems with such a course. Denying people an opportunity to express their lack of consent may be mistaken for acquiescence. Many commentators have taken the lack of any response to the Anglo-Irish accord as vigorous as that to Sunningdale in 1974 as showing that Ulster unionists have moderated considerably or had their spirit broken, and that, either way, the government can press down that road without fear of serious opposition. My guess is that such a strategy will be accepted only if it is accompanied by a complete cessation of IRA terrorism. It is possible to imagine unionists accepting a trade-off between their political rights and peace. However, to date every weakening of the position of unionists has been taken by the IRA as encouragement to more violence, not less.

But if we imagine some sort of settlement that is widely seen as a major change in Northern Ireland's position, how would the typical unionist respond? My answer has to be even more of a guess than my attempt to answer that question for the loyalists and evangelicals, but my assessment is that a willingness to fight for an independent smaller Ulster state is as common among Unionists as among loyalist paramilitaries and Democratic Unionists. Glen Barr's scheme for negotiated independence fell on deaf ears, but 'going it alone' remains the second best for most unionists.

One cannot put a percentage on it or specify at just what point of gradual expulsion from the United Kingdom such a response would be triggered, because, as a moment's thought will make clear, how active anyone would be in such a campaign would depend on the likelihood of it succeeding, and that in turn would be determined by many factors which could not be assessed until the time. I will say only that I have been frequently surprised by the willingness of people I had taken to be moderate unionists to say not only that they think fighting to remain free of a united Ireland would be legitimate but that they would be willing to join such a fight.

In 1983 a very detailed study of Belfast church-going Protestants asked people to respond to the statement 'If I ever had to chose between being loyal to the British government and being loyal to Ulster, I would always chose Ulster'. Despite the sample over-representing the views of middle-class Protestants, a full 60 per cent agreed. The more working-class attenders of mission halls were even more resolute: 80 per cent of them put loyalty to Ulster before loyalty to the government.[16]

5. THE POLITICS OF ETHNIC IDENTITY

MOST social-science writing on Northern Ireland fails to convey the bitter nature of the conflict and its residues. There is a good and a bad reason for this. The good reason is that social scientists are trying to illuminate and explain, not to shock. If we want a sense of what it feels like to hate and be hated, to threaten and feel threatened, then we should turn to fiction or to more journalistic accounts; Beattie's *We are the People* is a good example.[1] But there is a bad reason for the bloodlessness (and I choose that term deliberately) of much academic writing about Ulster and that is that many authors are committed to particular explanations of the Northern Ireland conflict which either play down sectarianism, or make it a property solely of loyalists, or both. In this chapter I will argue for the deeply sectarian nature of the conflict, consider the weaknesses of some popular approaches to the problem, and then offer an alternative and more realistically dismal portrayal of the Troubles.

BRITAIN'S BOSNIA

It is difficult for members of stable and liberal democracies to appreciate how easy it is for people to attack some other people simply because of their 'ethnicity'. In seeing the film footage of news reports from what used to be Yugoslavia we are horrified that Muslims will with little compunction murder Croats simply because they are Muslims, that Serbs will rape Bosnian Muslim girls repeatedly until they are pregnant and then gloat that they have turned the women's bodies into vehicles for their own oppression, and that neighbours who have for years lived together despite their differences will now kill because of them. We know that 'uncivilized' people in Africa do that sort of thing. Shona fight Ndebele in Zimbabwe; Zulu fight Xhosa in South Africa; Hutu fight Tutsi in Burundi. We might recall the murder of at least five million European Jews; the Holocaust was within the living memory of our parents, but none the less it seems to belong to an earlier world, a time when everything was in black and white. We have racist political movements, but these are very small and obviously peopled by low-IQ members of the lumpen proletariat. In our political culture, ethnic conflict is implausible, and even nationalist movements (such as the Scottish National Party (SNP)) tend to promote their cause on the grounds of democracy and efficiency rather than on notions of racial or ethnic purity and advantage. In 1993 the SNP expelled a group called Settler Watch for encouraging animosity towards 'white settlers' in rural Scotland.

Because ethnic conflict is rare, we make it rarer still by overlooking it when it does raise its head or by too readily accepting an alternative conceptualization of it. I do not want to argue that ethnic hostility has no economic and social causes—'the knee bone is connected to the thigh bone'—but I do want to suggest that accounts of the Northern Ireland conflict that concentrate on individual civil rights, imperial interests, and class to the exclusion of ethnicity miss an important point and I will begin that argument by looking at the ethnic nature of the violence of the Troubles.

The first serious attacks in the present wave of violence in Ireland were *communal*. In Belfast, Protestants attacked Catholic homes in Catholic streets in order to harm or drive out Catholics. Catholics did the same. Apologists for republicanism simply overlook the evidence. Bell, for example, laughably claims 'There was never any great element of sectarianism in the Provisionals' campaign.'[2] When the IRA launched its bombing campaign, the targets were not only representatives of the British state but ordinary Protestants. The bombs of 1971 were placed inside and outside pubs and clubs in Protestant areas and were only as selective as the establishments in question were 'select'. That is, they were intended to kill Protestants and they did just that. Bell twice mentions loyalists bombing Catholic pubs without mentioning that the Provisionals did it first.

The shift in security policy from having large numbers of British soldiers on the streets to increasing the size and capability of the RUC and the locally recruited Ulster Defence Regiment meant that the casualties of republican terror were increasingly Ulster Protestants (and, it should not be forgotten, some Catholics). This 'Ulsterization' of the conflict is sometimes presented as if it were a Machiavellian ploy by the British government to contain the casualties to Northern Ireland. There may well have been an element of that but to stress that point is to suggest quite inappropriately that it is the British government's fault that hundreds of Protestants have been killed by the IRA. It is not. It is the IRA's fault, and it seems quite sensible to suppose that, however much the political thinkers in the republican movement try to confine their violence in ways that make it easier to justify, IRA members like killing 'Orangies'. Consider the way in which the republican definition of a legitimate target expands to include not just serving members of the police and army but also retired members of the police and army, members of the families of policemen and soldiers, civilians who work for the security forces, publicans and shopkeepers who supply policemen and soldiers, and any civilian who happens to frequent any establishment with a service clientele (the girls who danced with off-duty soldiers at the Dropping Well pub in Ballykelly, for example). And with the Enniskillen bombing we have the addition of anyone who attends a memorial service to soldiers who died in wars quite unconnected with Northern Ireland. Given that it is hard to think of any category of Protestant excluded from the list, we have to suppose that Martin McGuinness's claim that 'there is no desire among genuine republicans to kill anyone in the Protestant community because of their religion'[3] can only be true because 'genuine republicans' have conveniently found other more PR-friendly reasons for killing pretty well everyone in the Protestant community.

While one purpose of republican violence is to terrorize people and so to destabilize the state (and for that, killing Catholic shoppers in Belfast city centre with massive car bombs is as useful as killing Protestants), another is to frighten Protestants into submission or out of the country. This explains not only the murder of individual Protestants in border areas but also such 'mass' attacks as the machine-gunning of Orangemen in an Orange Hall in Tullyvallen, Pentecostalists at worship in a gospel hall at Darkley, and Protestant workers in a minibus stopped at Kingsmills in South Armagh.

Whatever the particular stimulus to any of these attacks, they show a common hatred of the victims, not as individuals but as *members of a group*. In so far as republicans are more likely than loyalists to confine their killing to 'legitimate' targets, this is not because of any greater humanity but because so many Protestants are legitimate targets that the desire to kill Protestants is fully satisfied, and the capacity to kill fully utilized, without going beyond that very long list of candidates.

Loyalist violence is also primarily communal. In 1969 and 1970 working-class Protestants in Belfast burnt Catholics out of their homes. They enthusiastically adopted the IRA's pub-bombing strategy, and in one incident planted a bomb in a pub on the Whiterock Road and placed snipers to shoot at people fleeing the scene. Although leaders of the UDA and UVF have periodically tried to confine the violence of their members to some notion of 'legitimate targets' (that is, republicans) or have claimed to be trying so to restrict the deaths, very many of their victims were chosen simply because they were Catholics. Even in these more publicity-conscious days there are loyalist paramilitary leaders who say that they like to kill republicans but an ordinary Catholic will do.[4]

As further evidence of the fundamentally sectarian nature of the conflict, I would point to the proportionately very large number of attacks on those who betray their own people. That betrayal can take the form of publicly associating oneself with the politics or policies of the other side. Catholic RUC men are more popular victims for the IRA than are Protestants in the police. John Turnly was a popular victim for the UDA not because he was associated with the republican National H-Blocks

Committee and the Irish Independence Party but because he was a *Protestant* who was so associated. And for both sides 'touts' deserve killing because they are a practical threat to the organization and they are a symbolic affront to their own people. Even more so are those people who have married 'one of them'.

At least in public, many in Northern Ireland deny the communal nature of the violence. Often one finds people insisting that relations between Protestants and Catholics in their town or their area or their street were always good and that this murder or arson attack must have been the work of outsiders. Such contrasts of local harmony disrupted by demonic strangers were popular during the forced movements of population in 1970[5] and they are now regularly deployed to explain assassinations. Yet a consideration of the mechanics of many assassinations suggests a very different view of community relations. It is certainly true that, in many well-planned murders, the man (or men) who fires the guns is brought in from another area, but storage of the weapons, transport to and from the murder site, and a place to change clothes are often provided locally. And behind the six or seven people involved in the commission of any assassination, there are often local individuals who provide the information to identify and find the target. These are not members of paramilitary organizations but ordinary people who 'finger' those with whom they may have maintained the appearance of friendly relations for years. To give just one very recent example which could be multiplied endlessly, in October 1993 a 21-year-old Tyrone man pleaded guilty to conspiring to murder two workmates who were part-time soldiers in the Ulster Defence Regiment. Under pressure from the IRA, the young man had given details of the men's cars and their movements. His defence lawyer tried to minimize the man's involvement by arguing that he thought he was merely confirming what the IRA already knew, but he did nothing to warn his colleagues.[6] Or take the case of the employee of the Musgrave Park Hospital who gave IRA bombers access to a tunnel which allowed them to plant a powerful bomb and did nothing to raise the alarm.[7] Of course it is the case that many people are frightened into assisting terrorists, but there are far too many cases for me to avoid the conclusion that on each side there is a degree of dislike for the other side that belies the fine words about previously harmonious relations.

It only needs a little speculative arithmetic to appreciate the extent of collusion in violence. There are very many planned attacks which are aborted, which fail completely, or which leave victims wounded rather than dead. If we guess that the average 'successful' murder is accompanied by three failures, the more than 3,000 dead of the conflict to date must represent at least 10,000 planned murderous attacks. If one deducts from the population the very young and the very old, there are around 1 million people who could be involved in passing information to paramilitary gangs. This gives us a ratio of at least one planned attack for every 100 people. One could try the calculation with different and more detailed assumptions, but there is no getting away from the conclusion that, beyond the 4,000 or 5,000 who have been directly involved in paramilitary organizations, there are an awful lot of people who have had some part to play, no matter how small, in the casualties of the conflict.

Beyond that layer of responsibility, there must be an awful lot of people who would never dream of colluding in acts of violence yet who very privately, perhaps only to themselves, mutter 'Good on ya!' when one of 'them' gets 'smacked'.

In addition to the murders, which make the headlines and are remembered, there have been thousands of attacks on properties that belong to the other side and symbolize their hated culture and presence. Loyalists attack Catholic chapels, Catholic parochial schools and halls, GAA clubs, and Hibernian halls. Catholics attack Orange Halls and Protestant churches. Even those actions are only the tip of an enormous iceberg of petty intimidation. There is nothing at all unusual about the following example. Three young Catholics on an ACE scheme had recently started attending a one-day-a-week painting and decorating course at the Millfield campus of Belfast College of Technology. They were threatened by four men who told them that they had been watched: 'Now that we have got the three of you together you are not going to make it across Millfield at a quarter to five tonight.'[8]

Another recently publicized example that did not involve death threats can further illustrate the nature of community relations. A young Catholic secretary in a firm with an otherwise Protestant work-force was persistently victimized by one man who made frequent intimidatory remarks about Catholics and would leave newspaper stories of loyalist terror attacks on her desk. That was the work of one bigot, but it is interesting that no one else in the firm either challenged him or tried to protect the girl from such harassment.[9]

My conclusion from reading the reports of twenty-five years of violence, from mass murder to petty arson to casual threats, is that both peoples have one thing in common and that is their dislike of each other. Of course, neither collectivity is a homogeneous 'community'. Not all Protestants are unionists, not all unionists are loyalists, and not all loyalists wish harm to Catholics. Ditto for Catholics. It would be impossible to subdivide the groups so as to enumerate the people in each position and say with certainty what proportion dislikes the members of other side so much as to be willing to kill or to hurt or to discomfort them, but we can be sure that, on each side, there are very many people beyond the immediate circle of terrorists who feel that, in some sense or other, such attacks are justified or deserved or are 'the sort of thing you have to expect seeing the way they have treated us', and so on.

There may be important differences between Catholic and Protestant attitudes to violence. A group which sees its position improving—a rising if not yet risen people—may well express its loathing of the previously superior group in a manner different from the views of a group which sees itself on the slide and is fearful of losing even more. But that does not detract from the fundamental unity of the phenomenon of ethnic conflict.

One in five of the deaths of the Troubles have occurred in north Belfast. Yet one finds the MP for the area, Cecil Walker, saying: 'One of the things I've found is that the communities themselves have not become involved in violence. People in north Belfast have always worked together.'[10] It is easy to appreciate why public representatives have to put a cheerful face on things, but considering together the extent of the murder campaigns, the attacks on property, the casual violence, the collusion, and the intimidation makes ridiculous the habit of claiming good community relations.

The notion that the violence is primarily communal (or 'sectarian') and expresses deep ethnic animosity causes me to doubt the value of many common understandings of the Northern Ireland conflict. I will now briefly outline those doubts. For simplicity's sake, I have grouped a large number of approaches into just three. This will, of course, mean that many nuances are overlooked, but more detail can be found elsewhere[11] and need not concern us here.

THE NATIONALIST CASE

The classic nationalist view is that the present problems of Northern Ireland are a result of the colonial relationship between Britain and Ireland and hence will be solved by the withdrawal of the British from any part in the island of Ireland. Not only was Britain responsible for the presence of large numbers of Protestants in Ireland, but its continued involvement, most significantly in partitioning the island in 1920, prevents Ulster Protestants realizing where their best interests lie and appreciating their true identity, and allows them to exert an unwarranted veto on the sensible and inevitable development of a peaceful and prosperous and independent united Ireland. In this account, unionism and loyalism are the shallow and temporary product of the British colonial presence.

My first problem with this account is that it runs together past and present, so that an accurate depiction of the past is used to validate a misleading portrait of the present, which will cause us wrongly to predict people's actions. What matters is to recognize what sort of conflict we have *now*; in that task, history is not everything. One could reasonably describe the relationship between Britain and Ireland in the seventeenth and early eighteenth centuries as 'colonial', but of itself that does not mean that such an account is now accurate.

A simple test of the present appropriateness of the colonial story is to imagine the consequences of British withdrawal. Were the conflict a simple matter of a colony trying to rid itself of an occupying empire, then it would be resolved by the departure of the imperial power, as happened when metropolitan France finally abandoned Algeria. One does not have to be a unionist to question the parallel with Northern Ireland. 'Brits out' could be seen as the end of Britain's last colony, but it could also be described as the British government deciding it is no longer willing to protect its citizens in one corner of its realm from those who would annex that territory. The first description could be justified on the grounds that the citizens in question had no right to be in Ireland because they had been planted there three hundred years ago. We could insist that robbery requires restitution no matter how long ago it took place and that Britain still has no right to regard Ulster as part of its realm because it had no right to it three hundred years ago. That is a coherent position but it hardly helps our understanding of the nature of the present conflict. The obvious point is that the 'planting' took place so long ago that to base present political decisions on the reversibility of that history is as sensible as asserting that all whites other than those whose residence pre-dates the Pilgrim fathers should be expelled from the United States. The fact is that the Protestants in Northern Ireland have been there since before the white man saw off the American buffalo, see themselves as British, and are bitterly opposed to having their British citizenship removed.

The nationalist case supposes the shallowness of the British identity of Ulster Protestants. It is hoped that they will respond to their expulsion from Britain by fairly readily reconciling themselves to becoming something very different. Yet no evidence is ever offered for that hope and the sad irony is that the twenty-five years of republican violence have made that even more of a pitifully forlorn hope than it was in 1912 or in 1920 or in 1969. As some Sinn Feiners now concede, Ulster loyalists have a cohesion and a sense of identity which are not so fragile as to dissolve the moment the institutional support of British citizenship is removed, and the republican armed struggle has done nothing but strengthen it. This is the view that John Hume is trying to persuade the IRA to accept, but Martin McGuinness's December 1993 restatement of the principle that British withdrawal is the only solution to the problem suggests that he is not succeeding.[12]

THE MARXIST CASE

The same error of supposing Ulster loyalism to be precarious is also made by the many mostly academic commentators who suppose that the core of the Northern Ireland conflict is the uneven distribution of wealth and power to minority and majority peoples. The problem is essentially one of discrimination or structured inequality, and the removal of the institutional supports for such discrimination will expose the fragile nature of the shared identities that the minority and majority have developed (or, at least, it will for the latter). Again history is deployed. Speaking of the first two decades of this century, Farrell says: 'The Unionist leaders . . . had mobilised the Protestant masses to resist Home Rule and inclusion in the Free State, through a policy of discrimination and the ideology of Protestant supremacy.'[13] The implication, as Whyte notes, is that the Protestant working class, if it had not been stirred up by 'the policy of discrimination and the ideology of Protestant supremacy', would have been naturally Irish rather than British.[14] Desmond Bell takes a similarly economistic view: 'Protestant workers have sought to defend their marginal privileges through their participation in a Protestant all-class alliance ideologically and politically under-written by British imperialism.'[15] In Bell's version, Protestants are at least given the credit for pursuing their own interests and are not portrayed simply as dupes of the ruling class, but none the less economic interests are seen as being at the heart of Protestant unionism.

As in the colonial account, we need to be profoundly suspicious of the use of descriptions of the past to explain the present. Let us consider the nationalist side first. It may well be that the alienation of some Catholics from the British state resulted from the state's support for Protestant domination, but what follows in terms of policy? Will treating everyone fairly now erode support for Irish nationalism? At the margins it might. One can well suppose that a section of SDLP voters will become unionists if they find status differences between Protestants and Catholics reduced. However, this seems likely to have very little effect on those Catholics who support Sinn Fein or on those SDLP voters who are straightforward nationalists. After all, the core of their complaint is that they are in the wrong country, and that will presumably remain no matter how well they are treated in that country.

This seems so obvious that it is hard to understand how it could be missed, but missed it very often is. The US social scientist McClung Lee manages to write extensively about the oppression of Catholics in Northern Ireland without once alluding to the possibility that the IRA might continue its campaign and continue to be well supported in it, irrespective of what the British government does.[16] The same mistake is made by those analysts who blame the continuing violence on the failure of the British government sufficiently to reform the Northern Ireland state.[17] Irrespective of the extent of active discrimination against Catholics, to treat the Northern Ireland conflict as being essentially rooted in disparities of fortune between Catholic and Protestant is to miss the point that Irish nationalism predates partition. Economic disadvantage does not exhaust the list of nationalist grievances, and the major grievance—being in the wrong country—pre-dates the Stormont regime and British direct rule. It was partly satisfied with the removal of the first, but will only be fully satisfied with the destruction of the second.

Taken simply as a device for creating peace and stability (that is, irrespective of its many other merits), social reform is a double failure. Not only has its failed to win for the state the allegiance of many Catholics, but it has also alienated many Protestants. For a time before he led the 1916 Easter Rising in Dublin, the nationalist and socialist James Connolly agitated in Belfast. The story is told of one meeting he addressed in Library Street. He was interrupted by an Orangeman who waved a copy of the 1912 Solemn League and Covenant and declared that he and the thousands of his co-signatories would see to it that there was no home rule. 'Connolly, with a sardonic smile, advised him to take the document home and frame it, adding "Your children will laugh at it."'[18] We are now on to the great-grandchildren and there is not a lot of laughing. As I tried to explain in Chapter 2, the increasingly widespread belief that the British government is deliberately directing resources and policy to the benefit of the minority has strengthened loyalist resolve to resist a united Ireland (which would be the same in spades, because all the levers of public policy would be controlled by Irish Catholics). To the extent that British treatment of unionists has weakened their sense of simply 'being British', it has increased their sense of being Ulster loyalists.

THE LIBERAL CASE

The third account I wish to question is at first sight very different from the first two. Rather than supposing that unionism in its loyalist form is a fragile flower which will wilt when no longer tended by its British state patrons, the liberal approach to the Northern Ireland problem requires that unionism, framed in a particular way, is to be celebrated and vaunted.

The liberal supposes that (*a*) the concerns that apparently drive communal conflict should not motivate civilized people (and that moral 'should not' often drifts into an explanatory 'does not'); (*b*) the conflict is thus based on mutual misunderstanding; and (*c*) the solution lies in persuading the protagonists to redefine their concerns so that the ugly caterpillar of sectarianism is transformed into the beautiful and inoffensive butterfly of *tradition*.

The first point is important. One can make too much of this, but I am often struck by the feeling that English civil servants and politicians and academic commentators do not really understand loyalists or nationalists. Though they hear the words that are spoken, the concerns of which they speak are so foreign to the modern liberal mind that they are taken to be either an exaggeration of feeling or a disguise for something else. Throughout the Western world, since the 1960s we have seen a considerable rise in cynicism towards such old-fashioned concerns as national pride, but in the English case this has been added to a long tradition of apparently forgoing national self-interest. The English are rather disdainful of the fervent nationalism of the French or the Germans. One suspects this comes from having a long history of winning and of being free from foreign invasion. This is not to say that the English are unmindful of national interest, only that they have a style which disdains loud expressions of national identity as vulgar and crude. And the liberal is so firmly wedded to the individualism of modern industrial democracies that communal identities, be they religious, ethnic, or national, are regarded as prehistoric throwbacks.

Liberals get on well with each other. In such middle-class suburbs as the Malone Road area of Belfast, in such organizations as the Alliance Party, and in such associations as Protestant and Catholic Encounter, Protestant and Catholic liberals mix and find they have much in common. They are thus readily drawn to the idea that the conflict is caused by misunderstanding and ignorance. If working-class people also mixed, they would learn that their stereotypes are mistaken—'they' do not have horns— and that they are just like us. End of conflict.

There is a long tradition of supposing that Northern Ireland's segregated school system is a major part of the problem. In 1966 Prime Minister Terence O'Neill said: 'Many people have questioned . . . whether the maintenance of two distinct educational systems side by side is not wasteful of human and financial resources, and a major barrier to the promotion of mutual understanding.'[19] His ordering of the two deleterious consequences—efficiency before social identity—is itself reveal-ing. Although ending segregated education is politically impossible, the government now encourages the creation of integrated schools and has made compulsory two cross-curricular programmes—'Education for Mutual Understanding' and 'Cultural Heritage'. To quote from a Central Office for

Information booklet on Northern Ireland: 'Some £1.9 million is spent annually on a Cultural Traditions Programme, which is aimed at encouraging greater understanding of different cultural traditions in Northern Ireland and showing that differences do not have to lead to division.'[20] There are also many charities which run play and holiday schemes that bring Protestant and Catholic children together in the hope that they will come to see that whatever divides them is less important than their common humanity.

'Mix and fix' has a long history in the United States, where it was promoted as a solution to racial intolerance. It is worth noting that it has not been a great success in the States, despite there being two reasons why US racial tension should have been easier to resolve than the Protestant–Catholic conflict in Northern Ireland. First, blacks are asking only that the state live up to its liberal rhetoric in the allocation of rights and privileges; they are not trying to change the constitutional position of the country. Secondly, blacks and whites are competing within an expanding economy which means that white *relative* loss of position to blacks is not also an absolute loss.

There are two major weaknesses in such notions as 'Education for Mutual Understanding'. First, they assume that social conflict is an error. If nothing else, the wars in eastern Europe should have reminded us that group conflict can be entirely rational. We may not like what the Serbs are doing in Bosnia and we may hope that in the long run they will trip themselves up (their war destroying their domestic economy, for example), but there is no mystery about their motives. They believe that they will be happier in an ethnically pure, single-religion state, and that such a state can be made safer, richer, more powerful, and more influential if they conquer as much territory for it as they can; unpleasant but not irrational. The same holds at a sub-state level. There are perfectly sensible reasons for group identification and conflict; ethnicity is not an early morning fog that will evaporate under the bright light of rising understanding.

The second mistake of 'mix and fix' is to underestimate the importance of perceptions. If sociology has one central principle, it is the 'definition of the situation' enunciated by W. I. Thomas when he said that, if people define a situation as real, then it is real in its consequences.[21] We respond, not to the objective world, but to our perceptions of our world, and those perceptions will be heavily coloured by our culture, our past experiences, our present interests, and our future intentions. Furthermore, such responses are *social* as well as individual. A 'definition of the situation' is always easier to sustain when it is shared by everyone around you, or everyone who matters to you. Like most people, liberals know that but apply it inconsistently. So they believe that the extremists on each side of the conflict act as they do because their (wrong) perceptions colour their interpretations (and mislead them), but they also believe that some pleasant social contact across the communal divide and some education will change the erroneous stereotypes. People do change, but government-sponsored play schemes are hardly likely to weigh more powerfully than the visions of one's family, friends, streets, and people. In practical terms, as one very experienced researcher concluded, Northern Ireland's divisions are so deep that forced integration (in schooling, for example) will simply import into those settings the conflicts found outside.[22]

In its most sophisticated form, the liberal response involves not just persuading Protestants and Catholics to talk to each other (as if they did not already) but invites them to redefine what are seen as competing political aspirations so that they become something more like hobbies and leisure pursuits. In the forefront of this work is the Community Relations Commission's programme to promote 'two traditions'.

In reading the cultural-traditions literature[23] I am struck by instructive parallels with the logic of religious toleration in the ecumenical movement which I would like to pursue. Until the last quarter of the nineteenth century most British churches were exclusive and intolerant in ideology (even if not in practice, though many were both). Each believed that it and only it was correct. This attitude naturally made interdenominational co-operation difficult, if not impossible, yet the churches faced common problems: for example, working in mission fields, providing cost-effective training for clergy, shifting resources to follow population movements, or dealing with the state. The first co-operative ventures were conducted on the basis of what was called 'undenominationalism'. Each party simply overlooked the fact that the others were foolish enough to be Methodist rather than Presbyterian, or whatever. Christians were required to leave to one side those beliefs which divided them and co-operate on the basis of what they had in common. However, this clearly did not allow for a very wide ecumenical movement, because what the churches had in common was not much. Ignoring differences could allow varieties of Presbyterian to work together (if they wanted), even Baptists and Methodists, but the gap between these thoroughly Protestant groups and the only partly reformed Church of England was far too great to be bridged by such a strategy. An alternative was needed and it was found in relativism.

It has long been a foundation of Western rational thought that two contradictory propositions—I am sitting on a chair; I am not sitting on a chair—cannot simultaneously be true. One (or both— I may be lying down) must be false. The interdenominational position argued that competing traditions could be simultaneously valuable. Whether or not a denomination's beliefs were true or effective in achieving salvation was set aside in favour of talking about what was 'valuable' and 'instructive'. It was hoped, and it turned out this way, that, if attention could be diverted from competing elements for long enough and people allowed to enjoy both what they held in common and the novelty of each other's distinctiveness, then an implicit relativism would set in and Methodists and Anglicans would cease to regard their views as competing. If Methodism is true for you and Anglicanism is true for me, then, despite being quite different and in many points contradictory, they are both in some sense 'true'.

Initially the range of competing views that it was hoped so to encompass was narrow: essentially competing varieties of Protestantism. But this soon expanded to include Orthodoxy, Unitarianism, and then Roman Catholicism. What was being asked of Christians in the ecumenical movement was not that they abandon any of their beliefs (other than those related to the status of their beliefs and to the right response to error) but that they change the logical and psychological status of those beliefs so that they could continue to hold their own views while allowing others to hold incompatible views.

This is a valuable social strategy for dealing with differences. Instead of arguing about what divides us or giving up beliefs we value, we restrict the scope and range of those beliefs so that they apply only to us and our fellow believers. Beliefs and cultures become privatized in the sense of being thought to apply only to those who accept them. But there are limits to this strategy.

Words are cheaper than actions and some forms of action are a lot cheaper than others. One of the virtues of ecumenical relativism is that the required change can be confined to rhetoric. The committed evangelical may find it hard even to accept a language which allows that Roman Catholicism is a different but equally valid form of Christianity, but very many Protestants could because such an acceptance did not require them to do anything much. They did not have to become Catholics. If they did not want to, they did not have to share services with a Catholic priest. Changes could be confined to public rhetoric (private speech could remain unchanged) and formal relations between officers of the appropriate bureaucracies.

The logic of ecumenism is that differences need not divide people. My response is 'that depends on the subject-matter of the differences'. In most parts of modern Britain, religion is a voluntary activity confined to the home, the family, and the leisure sphere. Differences here can readily be accommodated without serious social divisions because one person's choices have very few consequences for anyone else's. That is, ecumenism is possible in a society which has relegated religion to the private world or, to put it crudely, in a world which is not very religious. The obvious parallel in Northern Ireland is the observation that integrated education works well for that relatively small number of families who are not strongly committed to a particular ethnic identity and a particular side in the conflict.

There is also a difference between the subject-matter of religion and that of politics. Religion is about the super-natural, and in that realm such rules of the natural world as non-contradiction need not apply. Without going so far as accepting the Hindu and Buddhist belief that all differences are superficial and that fundamentally 'all is one', the religious person can believe that different religious beliefs and practices all contain something that glorifies God. After all, God is all-powerful, and so allowing people to find him through both the florid Catholic Mass and the Quaker shared silence should not be beyond his capacities. If not all roads lead to God, it is still possible to believe that God can defy the normal rules of geography. Arrangements in the material world are not so readily susceptible to that sort of reasoning. The sceptic may expect to be as badly off under any political system, but even he will not see democracy and autocracy as being 'interestingly different facets' of the same thing. Very small numbers of people can be allowed to be citizens of two countries, but sovereignty is indivisible. Ulster cannot simultaneously be part of the United Kingdom and of the Republic of Ireland. Or, at least, if it was jointly ruled (whatever that could mean), it would be in quite a different position from the rest of both of those states. Joint sovereignty is not the simultaneous satisfaction of unionist and nationalist programmes; it is a third quite different programme.

The wonder of the cultural-traditions school is that it fails to appreciate that the relativism which can be permitted in thinking about religious divisions or dress styles cannot work in the obdurate world of constitutional politics. In February 1993 the intergovernmental conference set up under the Anglo-Irish accord produced another of its anodyne statements of good intention: 'Ministers reasserted their shared determination to provide a comprehensive political settlement which would address all the main relationships. They underlined their belief that such a settlement is attainable without requiring either of the two main traditions to sacrifice their interests or to prejudice their aspirations.'[24] As one loyalist responded when I cited that text: 'I'd like some of what they've been smoking!' Clearly Northern Ireland cannot be in two states and two jurisdictions simultaneously. It follows that the aspirations of nationalists and of unionists cannot simultaneously be met. Worse, because they are not only incompatible but competing, coming closer to satisfying one means further disappointing the other.

The key to understanding how presumably sensible people could so delude themselves as to sign such a statement lies in the hope implied in the word 'tradition'. I am not sure of its origins in Ulster political parlance, but it is quite recent and it is favoured by nationalists and liberals, though for very different reasons. Nationalists like it because it implies that Ulster politics should not be determined by the weight of individual voters. Nationalists, a minority, are put on a par with unionists (a very clear and large majority); both traditions are equally valid. The term has the added advantage of avoiding the republican connotation of 'people'. To talk of the 'Irish people' is just a bit too openly nationalist. What attracts the liberal is the hope that, by defining the competing political agendas of the ethnic groups as traditions, the relativism trick of the ecumenical movement will be pulled off. A tradition sounds nice and cuddly, something for the tourist and heritage industries. Unionism is neutered to bright banners, bowler hats, and Somme memorials; nationalism is reduced to whistle music, knitted sweaters, stout, and turf fires. The notion of tradition also contains the hope that the political desires of those peoples will be fixed in the past and thus prevented from contaminating the future. Nationalists and unionists are now to celebrate the history of their political differences but not pursue their different interests in the present. A marvellously silly example of this is the Opsahl Commission's recommendation that: 'We encourage those church members in the Orange Order and other similar bodies to use their influence to persuade these organizations to consider imaginative alternatives—such as summer festivals—to marches along "traditional" routes through areas which are now predominantly Catholic.'[25] One speaker at a Cultural Traditions Group conference said: 'There seems to be broad recognition that distinctiveness—even separateness—need not be equivalent to divisiveness.'[26] When the distinctiveness refers to competing political agendas and when the main item on those agendas— sovereignty—is indivisible and when there is an unspoken item on the agenda of many which is 'make the bastards pay for what they have done to my people', then distinctiveness does seem very obviously equivalent to divisiveness.

What might shift the sticking-point of competing constitutional desires is a radical change in the way we think about sovereignty. So long as the issue for people in Northern Ireland is to which of two nation states they belong, the two traditions must be competing. But, if the claims made on their citizens by nation states were weakened by an increase in the power of a supra-nation-state unit (in this case the European Union) and by an increase in regional autonomy, the possibilities of treating as 'equally valid' unionism and nationalism increase. This partly explains John Hume's fondness for Europe. We see it in the SNP's recent promotion of the slogan 'Scotland in Europe'. We see it in the Downing Street declaration.

Sadly for such hopes, the early 1990s have seen a step backwards from European integration. The European monetary system has collapsed. The GATT negotiations spent years bogged down in a welter of competing national interests. The recession has seen every European government pursuing its own interests at the expense of its neighbours. Even the Germans, long promoters of closer European integration, are now having doubts as they struggle to deal with the many problems of reuniting their country. Though the Maastricht treaty survived, it seems likely that it will be the British interpretation—a free-trade zone—rather than the Delors vision of European integration that will predominate.

The difficulties with the liberal approach to the Northern Ireland problem can be readily summarized. As individuals, unionists and nationalists in Ulster can be treated with equal respect by the British state, just as they are in Scotland. Group cultural differences can be treated as equally valid, again as they are in Scotland, where considerable amounts of public money are spent on Gaelic broadcasting. There are arguments about just how much money it is fair to spend on a linguistic and regional group of a certain size, but the principle is not disputed by most people. It may be foolish for a state to do so, but it is even possible to permit groups with a political agenda which calls for the destruction of the state to present that agenda and seek public support for it. But what it is not possible to do is simultaneously to satisfy two competing constitutional agendas, because that is not a matter of will or wisdom but of logic.

THE ETHNIC CONFLICT CASE

Smith offers the following depiction of an 'ethnic group': 'An ethnic group . . . is distinguished by four features: the sense of unique group origins, the knowledge of a unique group history and belief in its destiny, one or more dimensions of collective cultural individuality, and finally a sense of unique collective solidarity.'[27] In a more recent work, Smith says much the same thing in different words when he defines an ethnic group as 'a type of cultural collectivity, one that emphasises the role of myths of descent and historical memories, and this is recognised by one or more cultural differences like religion, customs, language or institutions'.[28] It seems very clear to me that Ulster Protestants form an ethnic group and that the Northern Ireland conflict is an ethnic conflict (Irish nationalism being a particular form of ethnic identification). Although appreciating those two facts does not provide a solution to the conflict, it allows us to avoid some serious errors in our understanding of it.

There are a number of objections to this view, some political, some based on a misunderstanding of what is being said, and I will now address these. First, what matters for ethnic identity is what people *believe* to be the case, not what actually is the case. We could now show that the shared belief in the purity of common descent is exaggerated and that Protestant settlers did marry Catholic natives, but this tells us only that the ethnic group is wrong in its beliefs, not that we are wrong in seeing an ethnic group.

Similarly, what matters about the historical memories of an ethnic group is not their correctness but their existence. We can use our knowledge of the historical record to show that the ethnic group is rewriting the past so that its present concerns and lines of demarcation appear as an inevitable consequence of its heroic past, but this will not alter the cohesion of the group nor the role of the mythical past. This is the sad pointlessness of historical nit-picking. To show, as deriders of Orangeism are very fond of doing, that the Pope was actually on the side of King William in the seventeenth century is not going to cause present-day Ulster Protestants to throw up their hands and announce 'Sorry, we have got it wrong!' Reminding Presbyterians that at the time of the United Irishmen movement many Ulster Presbyterians were on the same side as Irish Catholics is not going to cause present-day Orangemen to discover common identity with Sinn Fein. Contesting, as writers of Letters to the Editor are fond of doing, the right of the UDA to the adjective 'Ulster' on the grounds that three of the nine counties of the old province are in the Republic is not going to save a single murder victim.

Benedict Anderson entitled his classic work on nationalism *Imagined Communities*.[29] The point he was making was the simple one that any community that includes more than this generation and a larger number of people than one can know personally cannot just exist but must be created and maintained by ideas, by beliefs about its existence. In so far as there is an 'Irish people', it is because putative members of that collectivity believe that they have important things in common which distinguish them from other people. In that sense, pretty well every group bigger than the extended family is an imagined community, as is any collectivity which regards the past (and hence members now deceased) as important. Anderson's phrase is useful in reminding us that collectivities require ideological work; members need to create and maintain myths. But it is slightly dangerous in that it may be supposed that what is imagined can be readily imagined *away*. As I have tried to argue, this is a key weakness of many approaches to Northern Ireland. While commentators are willing to accord substance to 'the Irish people' and thus treat Irish nationalism as something which has to be accommodated, they are often prone to seeing Ulster loyalism as far less durable: brought into being by recent political structures, and liable to dissolve when its powerful imperial promoters withdraw their patronage. Smith is absolutely correct to argue against those people (usually spokesmen for a particular 'nation' or 'ethnie') who want to see such bodies as primordial, inevitable, or natural, entities just waiting to be discovered. They are not. As the de-bunkers often point out, such groups constantly change, but in any time and place they can set the terms within which people act and think. No matter how much the more articulate republican spokesmen explain their violence in terms which try to avoid treating Protestants as a competing ethnic group, much republican terror is ethnic in its focus. 'Brits out' means 'Prods out'. For all that UDA and UVF leaders insist that ordinary Catholics have nothing to fear from them, most loyalist violence is directed against Catholics because they are Catholics.

The depth of the ethnic divisions in Northern Ireland is such that it is almost impossible to think, and harder to act, in any other terms. Policies which are devised on individualistic lines ('fair employment', for example) quickly become ethnic head-counting. Even if they are not intended as such, the consequences are always assimilated to a Manichean model of them and us. The Housing Executive tries to allocate housing on the basis of individually defined needs and because the individuals in question act ethnically (by wanting to live among their own people); the consequence is that housing distribution becomes ethnically charged. Houses for the increasing Catholic population mean territory taken from Protestants.

Even approaches to the problem which present themselves as innovative readily fall into thinking on ethnic-group lines. 'Initiative '92', which led to the Opsahl Commission, was promoted as an attempt to find radical new lines for political development by soliciting the widest possible representations and then subjecting them to the radical scrutiny of the bright but disinterested. Its report frequently refers to the dangers of stereotyping Northern Ireland people as being simply Catholic or Protestant, nationalist or unionist, but then recommends that 'each community has an equal voice in making and executing the laws or a veto on their execution and equally shares administrative authority'.[30] This, of course, requires that all people identify themselves with an ethnic group and act on the basis of ethnic self-interest.

If ethnic divisions are often inadvertently reinforced by policies designed to ignore them, how much more are they firmly entrenched by policies which take for granted their salience. The two major political innovations in Northern Ireland—the power-sharing Executive of 1974 and the Anglo-Irish accord of 1985—were both designed to recognize ethnic division. Under the Sunningdale agreement power was to be shared by people who were only incidentally representatives of political parties; primarily they were representatives of their ethnic groups. The Executive was every bit as much an ethnic carve-up as that of the 1943 Lebanese constitution which requires the President to be a Maronite Christian, the Prime Minister to be a Sunni Muslim, the Speaker of the National Assembly to be a Shia Muslim, and the Chief of Staff of the Armed Forces to be a Druze. The Anglo-Irish accord, despite being an agreement between two liberal democracies, approaches the problem of Northern Ireland not in terms of the rights and privileges of individuals but in terms of the rights and privileges of ethnic collectivities.

As I have already said, our ethnicity is always just one of a number of identities we can call upon. The extent to which we give it priority over our family, work group, neighbourhood, profession, hobby group. or whatever depends a great deal on the circumstances in which we have to live. It should be very obvious that ethnic warfare forces people to attend to their ethnicity. Until Bosnia-Herzegovina declared its independence and some Bosnian Serbs and Croats decided to associate with their sister ethnic states, many of the Muslims of Bosnia did not regard their ethnic identification as their most important characteristic. Once they found their co-religionists being killed because they were Muslims, that identity became vital. The violence in Northern Ireland has not yet reached the level where all the fences one might want to sit on have been replaced by fifteen-foot-high peace-line walls. Many middle-class Protestants and Catholics manage to remain relatively uninvolved, but even they cannot entirely escape being judged and reacted to on the basis of their perceived ethnic identification.

Let us return to murder. The responses to violent death have become perfectly predictable. With more forgiveness than many of us could manage, the families of victims announce that they do not want revenge. No one should suffer what they have had to suffer. Journalists and politicians announce that this new death makes it all the more important that a solution should be found. But, at the same time, each new death gets added to the mental list on which each community records the evidence of the essential evil of the other side. At one level everyone knows that the terrorists are only a small section of each community. At another, everyone suspects that a much larger group of people is implicated in some degree. But the logic of ethnic conflict is to generalize and to spread blame widely. For loyalists, the IRA is part of a pan-nationalist front. Even when people are selected as victims for reasons other than their ethnicity, they are seen by their own community as having died for that reason. Republicans may have killed Lord Mountbatten, Airey Neave, Ian Gow, Edgar Graham, Robert Bradford, and Sir Norman Stronge because they symbolized the British state, but Ulster Protestants see those as representatives of their government and their people. For nationalists, the UDA and UVF are agents of the British state, but at the level of popular appreciation they are 'Jaffas' and 'Orangies', representatives of all Ulster Protestants.

The point does not need labouring. The history of politics in the north-east of Ireland is a history of increasingly serious ethnic divisions. In a 1968 survey, the three labels of 'British', 'Irish', and 'Ulster' were chosen with equal frequency. In 1992 two-thirds of Protestants but only one in ten Catholics called themselves British. Three out of five Catholics but only one in fifty Protestants called themselves 'Irish'.[31] The 1991 census revealed a degree of residential segregation that surprised even many people in Northern Ireland. Half the population now lives in areas that are more than 90 per cent Protestant or 95 per cent Catholic. Irrespective of what part has been played in deepening the divisions by inept or inequitable security policy, economic management, and social administration, the ethnic division cannot now be imagined away, if ever it could have been. Nor can it be neutered by redefining it as a matter of different but equally valuable 'traditions', because these traditions are merely one manifestation of presently competing political agendas.

THE FUTURE

It is one thing to explain the nature of the Northern Ireland Troubles as an ethnic conflict. It is another thing to offer any hope of resolution. I would like now to summarize those of the preceding points in this book that have policy implications. So that the thoroughly dismal tone is maintained to the end, I will begin by repeating an observation I made in *God Save Ulster*:

What has been correctly understood by both republicans and loyalists, but overlooked by analysts and successive Westminster governments, is that there is no Northern Ireland 'problem'. The word 'problem' suggests that there is a 'solution': some outcome which will please almost everybody more than it displeases almost everybody. Conflict is a more accurate term for Protestant/Catholic relationships in Northern Ireland. Conflicts have outcomes, not solutions. Somebody wins and somebody loses.[32]

Reasoning about how to respond to deep ethnic divisions can go in two directions: to accept the ethnic fault lines where they lie and 'back a side', or to try to engineer circumstances that will reduce the salience of ethnic identity. So that we can appreciate the size of the second task, it is worth reminding ourselves of just how solid are the competing identities. The above figures on ethnic identification and residential segregation can be augmented with observations about party support.

At least 80 per cent of Catholics who vote vote for a nationalist party. Some 10 per cent vote for Sinn Fein and the rest vote for the SDLP. We know from opinion polls that a proportion of Catholics (it may be as high as 25 per cent) do not want a united Ireland in the foreseeable future, but it is clear that they continue to support a party which is no less nationalist than it was in 1974 and arguably more so. Then the SDLP settled for a Council of Ireland talking shop. Now it insists on Dublin involvement in the administration of Northern Ireland. Almost all Protestants who vote vote for a unionist party. Both the UUP and the DUP have shifted since 1974 in that they are more willing now to accept political structures for Northern Ireland which would prevent unionists enjoying the unfettered supremacy they enjoyed prior to

1972. However, the resilience of the DUP vote means that, even if there were in the UUP significant numbers who were willing to accept Dublin involvement, they could not promote such a course without losing very large numbers of votes to the more orthodox DUP. Anyway, it seems clear to me that there does not need to be a DUP hovering over the UUP's shoulder to keep it honest. There is no one in the UUP who is both willing to play the part of Brian Faulkner and able to command enough support to make it worth his while.

There are, of course, many people in Ulster who do not wish to identify strongly with either nationalist or unionist cause. However, the very fact of conflict gives them little option, and structures have an independent effect of exaggerating ethnic identification. The many Catholics who do not want a united Ireland in the near future (and possibly not at all) cannot desert the SDLP without by default strengthening the position of the unionists. Further, as the conflicts in eastern Europe clearly show, the more violence and instability there is, the more difficult it is to remain in a neutral position. War does not just mobilize those people who want war; it sucks in everybody. The high proportion of middle-class Catholics who are a little detached from the nationalist agenda suggests that neutrality is easier for them than for unionists, and this is what we would expect. All the changes of the last twenty-five years have been in the direction of weakening the position of unionists and the place of Northern Ireland in the United Kingdom. It is easier for those who feel they are winning anyway, than for those who are losing, to be a little detached from the game.

It might be possible to reduce both the numbers committed to these antagonistic positions and the strength of their resolve, and this has been the main thrust of government policy, but it has been done in an extremely partial manner. In so far as the actions of the British government have weakened Protestant attachments to unionism, it has been through stick rather than carrot. Though the gradual incorporation of Dublin has been presented as complementing the 'British' position of Northern Ireland rather than undermining it, the fact that sovereignty is seen by almost everyone involved as a 'zero-sum' game means that the political changes are seen by unionists as all loss and no compensation. And, as I have noted a number of times, the weakening of Ulster British identity has strengthened the Ulster loyalist identity and thus made reconciliation between Catholics and Protestants less, rather than more, likely.

It is difficult to be as sure of the effects of British attempts to wean Catholics away from hard-line nationalism. The rise of Sinn Fein in the 1980s and its persistence despite continued IRA murder and mayhem suggest that they have not been terribly successful. As I have also noted a number of times, it is clear that one consequence of redistributive social policy (irrespective of any effect on Catholic disadvantage) has been further to alienate unionists. Sadly, this seems an inevitable consequence of the structure of division in the province. Every specific action or programme is appropriated by one side or the other and assimilated to the vision of ethnic competition. Any initiative designed to ameliorate poverty, for example, will be regarded by one side as insufficient and by the other as too much. Any political changes designed to induce Catholic support for the British government (either in its role as master of 'direct rule' or as guarantor of a regional structure) will give Catholics either too little or too much for unionists to tolerate, and most of the time will do both. This, of course, is not an argument against equitable social policy and administration; it is simply a caution against hoping that such changes will resolve the political problem.

If this reasoning is not too pessimistic, it leads us to conclude that the ethnic divisions are now so deep as to be beyond manipulation. What then of the alternative approach, of simply backing a side? If, as seems very likely, the IRA does not accept the invitation of the Downing Street declaration and renounce violence, the British government could call a halt to any speculation about the constitutional position of Northern Ireland. It could abandon all talk of change coming when there is a majority for change and insist that there will not be any change. Such an assurance would, I suspect, confirm the resolve of the republican movement to pursue the armed struggle, but, if it was widely supposed that the government was serious, it might slightly reduce active support for the IRA: movements recruit better when there is a chance of success than when the goal is unattainable. It is difficult to guess the response of nationalists outside the republican movement, but, so long as a firm stand on the constitution is accompanied by social and economic changes that allow the continued growth of the Catholic middle class, and by an increase in local government or regional powers that allow Catholics to exercise power within Northern Ireland, then the proportion of Catholic unionists might increase slightly. However, again we come back to the way in which the nature of the political structures of the conflict reduce the freedom for deviation from its fundamental fault lines. Increased power for councils would give more say in the running of Northern Ireland to Catholics west of the River Bann, but, as constitutional Catholic political expression is through the nationalist SDLP, such changes would increase the power and influence of a party committed to further weakening of the Union.

Unionists would certainly be satisfied with an end to constitutional speculation and innovation. Some working-class loyalists would still be motivated to violence by the continued republican campaign and by redistributive social and economic policies, but one can imagine general support for the UDA and UVF shrinking back to the level of the mid-1980s. To summarize, a firm commitment to the status of Northern Ireland within the United Kingdom and an end to Dublin involvement in the province would probably leave things much as they are now.

The British government could decide to back the other side. The more jaundiced unionists suppose that this is already government policy:

Major says he is not going to be a 'persuader' for a united Ireland. What the fuck does he think the government has been since 1969? The sugar plum fairy? The Tories took away the B Specials, they took away Stormont, they pissed on every bloody proposal the unionist majority made. Thatcher sends my son and thousands of other squaddies to defend fifty sheep shaggers on the far side of the globe and then signs us away in the Anglo-Irish accord. If that is not acting as a persuader for the Free State then what the fuck is it?

Though usually less trenchantly expressed, such views are common among unionists, but, even if one accepts the general point that the (perhaps unintended) consequence of British policy has been to further the nationalist agenda, the government has not yet committed itself to a united Ireland. London could now do as the SDLP wants and become one of the 'persuaders' for a united Ireland. It could go further and do as the IRA wants by becoming an enforcer.

The likelihood of London accepting the nationalist agenda presumably depends on British interpretations of self-interest, and we can consider some of the principles that will obviously guide such interpretations. First, it is worth noting that such a course is probably unprecedented in the history of modern nation states. States have been forced to give independence to their colonies. The disintegration of the British Empire, the more recent collapse of the Portuguese empire, and the continuing unravelling of what was the Soviet Union are all examples. But I cannot think of a case of a state willingly giving land and population to a neighbouring and already independent sovereign state. That it has not happened often enough for an example to occur to me suggests there are very powerful state interests which are not served by such generosity with national territory.

A second problem is the cost to Britain's international reputation that would result from the very dramatic and public loss of face involved in anything which could be interpreted as an IRA victory. Imagine how the government would feel about a *Time* magazine cover with a photograph of Adams and the headline 'IRA Victory in Ulster'.

A third problem is that the Republic of Ireland is in no position to take over and manage a Northern Ireland with more than half a million unhappy unionists. Those people who think unionism a shallow and temporary identity do not expect much opposition to forced unification. Farrell states their case neatly:

At the moment Britain supplies two-thirds of the full-time forces in the North and arms and pays for the rest as well as providing massive subsidies to run the area. With this backing it is easy to be intransigent. Deprived of these forces and subsidies and faced with the choice of

accepting a united Ireland or fighting to establish a permanently
beleaguered Protestant state, few Protestants are likely to chose the
latter.[33]

This sanguine view was not shared by the SDLP in 1988. In an
exchange of papers with Sinn Fein, the SDLP raised the issue of
the position of the RUC and the UDR (now the Royal Irish
Regiment) in the vacuum left by the announcement of British
withdrawal: 'Is it not likely and natural in the emotionally
charged atmosphere that would obtain and in the absence of any
acknowledged authority, that they would simply identify with the
community from which most of them come and become its
military defenders?'[34] In less apocalyptic style, John Whyte
made the point: 'Quite small numbers of extremists on each side
can force a situation where . . . the peacefully inclined majority
are obliged to seek protection from, and then give support to, the
paramilitaries of their own community.'[35] My cautious estima-
tion, at the end of the previous chapter, was that Whyte is closer
to the truth than Farrell. It is a simplification, of course, but many
signs point to the likeliest result of a British withdrawal being
merely a continuation of the conflict with the major roles
reversed. A change of cast would have the advantage for Britain
of passing over to the Republic responsibility for managing the
crisis, but it has the disadvantage that any considerable increase
in levels of violence in Ireland might well cause ripples in the
west of Scotland and the north-west of England. Instability in a
neighbouring state might be preferable to instability on the
margins of the national territory, but the gains might be slight.

Furthermore, even in the circumstance of relatively little
resistance, there will still be considerable costs to the Republic
and recent polls have suggested that not many people in the Irish
Republic are willing to incur any costs for a united Ireland.[36]

WHAT IS TO BE DONE?

Only the most committed partisan nationalist or loyalist could see
either of the routes laid out above as 'solving the problem'.

Anyone in the least bit detached from either camp should appreciate that a victory for either side will only deepen the distress of the other. None the less, if one accepts that positive social policy, no matter how beneficial in its own right, will not significantly reduce the ethnic divide, then one has to pick a side. Which side should the government choose?

As a relatively disinterested observer, I can suggest only one way of answering that question: calculate the numbers of those people who are presently British citizens (the government has no immediate responsibility for anyone else) who would be left most happy by either course. At present, and for the foreseeable future, Protestants will be a majority of the citizens of Northern Ireland and, near as makes no difference, all Protestants are unionists. In addition, many Catholics are unionists with a very small 'u'. In the 1993 local council elections there were twice as many unionists as nationalists elected. It follows that, in so far as one can separate out views about the constitutional position of Northern Ireland from a complex of other concerns about the ethnic division, doing the will of the majority leads one to the unionist rather than the nationalist position.

APPENDIX

TABLE 1. *Republican and loyalist murders 1969–1993*

Year	Republican	Loyalist	Year	Republican	Loyalist
1969	4	2	1982	73	10
1970	18	2	1983	51	9
1971	93	21	1984	43	8
1972	257	103	1985	45	2
1973	129	81	1986	41	16
1974	99	93	1987	69	17
1975	100	114	1988	65	22
1976	142	113	1989	40	21
1977	70	25	1990	46	19
1978	55	8	1991	47	42
1979	90	15	1992	36	39
1980	50	13	1993	35	47
1981	77	11			

Note: It has not always been possible to determine who was responsible for a particular murder. Many victims are claimed, either at the time or later, but others have to be attributed. Sometimes this can be done from a conviction or plea in court; sometimes one has to guess on the basis of the nature of the victim and the location of the murder. Analysts may differ in how they deal with 'own goals' and how they record the death of someone who succumbs in one year to an injury sustained in an earlier year. All of this means that there may be slight discrepancies between one published set of data and another. However, the number of disputed murders is a very small part of the total and one can have confidence in the broad patterns.

Source: Data for 1969–88 supplied by Irish Information Partnership; data for 1989–93 supplied by RUC Information Office.

FIGURE 1. *Republican and loyalist murders 1969–93*

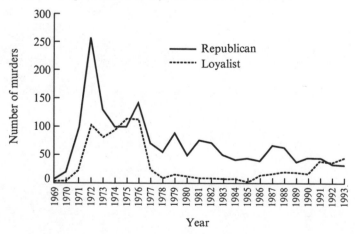

Source: As for Table 1.

Notes

CHAPTER 1. GUNMEN AND EVANGELICALS

With the exception of quotations from certain documents of unquestionable provenance, such as the current constitution of the Irish Republic, all quotations in the text that are not followed by a source listed below are from interviews I conducted in 1992 and 1993.

1. The term 'Unionist', with an initial upper case, is reserved for members or supporters of the Ulster Unionist Party (UUP).
2. J. Todd, 'Two Traditions in Unionist Political Culture', *Irish Political Studies*, 2 (1987), 1–26.
3. The Ulster Young Militants (UYM), Ulster Defence Force (UDF), and Ulster Freedom Fighters (UFF) are names used by sections of the UDA. The Young Citizens' Volunteers (YCV) and the Protestant Action Force (PAF) are sections of the UVF. The Red Hand Commando (RHC) was formed by John McKeague after he was pushed out of the early UDA; it later became closely associated with the UVF. For other loyalist groups, see n. 7.
4. For an excellent readable history of the first UVF, see P. Orr, *The Road to the Somme* (Belfast, 1987).
5. For details of violence in 1920 and 1921, see M. Farrell, *Arming the Protestants: The Formation of the Ulster Special Constabulary and the Royal Ulster Constabulary, 1920–27* (London, 1983), and *Northern Ireland: The Orange State* (London, 1980); and A. Hezlet, *The 'B' Specials: A History of the Ulster Special Constabulary* (London, 1972).
6. M. Dillon, *The Shankill Butchers: A Case Study of Mass Murder* (London, 1989), 39. For a more detailed history of the loyalist paramilitaries, see S. Bruce, *The Red Hand: Protestant Paramilitaries in Northern Ireland* (Oxford, 1992).
7. A small number of middle-class people and farmers were involved in 'respectable' paramilitary organizations such as the Ulster

Special Constabulary Association, the Vanguard Service Corp (which was linked to Craig's Vanguard), the Ulster Service Corp (which recruited ex-B Specials) and the Orange Volunteers. These did little violence but sometimes marched, sometimes collected weapons, and helped organize the 1974 strike.

8. Much controversy is provoked by the supposed moral and political implications of the description of loyalist violence as 'counter-terrorism'. It is a small technical point, but I do not use that description for the UDA and UVF because it relates loyalist violence too closely to republican *violence*. In *The Red Hand* I prefer the term 'pro-state terrorism' because it relates loyalist violence to perceived threats to the state. For a discussion of analytically linked contrasts between pro-state and anti-state terrorism, see S. Bruce, 'Pro-State Terror: Loyalist Paramilitaries in Northern Ireland', *Terrorism and Political Violence*, 4 (1992), 67–88.

9. J. McVeigh, *A Wounded Church: Religion, Politics and Justice in Ireland* (Cork, 1989), 76.

10. A very different view (and one hard to sustain from the chronology) is given by IRA volunteer Shane O'Doherty when he writes: 'Catholic pubs were being bombed without warning by Protestant paramilitaries, and IRA units retaliated by targeting Protestant pubs frequented by Protestant paramilitaries' (S. O'Doherty, *The Volunteer: A Former IRA Man's True Story* (London, 1993), 195). The Mountainview Tavern was frequented by UVF men only to the same extent that McGurk's was frequented by IRA men; they were working-class bars supposed to have a clear sectarian clientele.

11. M. Dillon and D. Lehane, *Political Murder in Northern Ireland* (London, 1973), was written with the express purpose of correctly attributing responsibility for the many murders of the early 1970s but offers inadvertent testimony to the difficulties of sorting out the dead by making mistakes, as Dillon himself later recognized; see M. Dillon, *The Dirty War* (London, 1990).

12. For an account of the Executive and UWC strike which powerfully conveys the feel of the period, see R. Fisk, *The Point of No Return: The Strike which Broke the British in Ulster* (London, 1975).

13. Yorkshire Television, *First Tuesday: 'Hidden Hand'*, transmitted 6 July 1993. There are a number of sources for the idea that the intelligence services were unhappy with Harold Wilson's Labour government, but the extension of that general claim into a specific

assertion that they deliberately set out to undermine the government's policy in Northern Ireland seems to come from just one source, though it has been repeated a number of times. The original source is Colin Wallace, a civilian employed at Army HQ in Lisburn in the early 1970s for press liaison and for the production of 'black' propaganda; see P. Foot, *Who Framed Colin Wallace?* (London, 1990). The general claim that the SAS was assisting the UVF in mid-Ulster comes from Fred Holroyd; see F. Holroyd, with N. Burbridge, *War without Honour* (Hull, 1989). There is not space here to examine the claims, but it is worth noting that Martin Dillon, David McKittrick, and I have all been over this ground and have not been persuaded by Wallace and Holroyd; see Bruce, *Red Hand*, ch. 8. It is also worth noting that their fulsome accounts of security-force ill-doing published only three and four years before the YTV film was made make no mention of security-force involvement in the Dublin and Monaghan bombs. However, that did not prevent *First Tuesday* using film of both men making vague or different accusations to lend the appearance of substance to their claims about those bombs.

14. Foot (*Who Framed Colin Wallace?*, 353–5) reports the involvement of one James Miller in the UDA. Miller was an Englishman living in Newtownabbey who claims to have worked for MI5 and to have been asked by his case officers to stimulate demands for a strike. He held no significant rank or influence in the organization and his encouragement would have been neither here nor there given the desire of very many far more senior paramilitaries for a strike.

15. The UDA was organized into areas which were called 'brigades', even though the number of members and the strength of structure never reached the levels normally associated with that notion. Usually there were four Belfast brigades (West, East, North, and South) and three others: Derry, Mid-Ulster, and South-East Antrim. The leaders of these units, plus the Supreme Commander (sometimes augmented by an overall military commander and senior political spokesmen, if they were not already there by virtue of being brigadiers), made up the Inner Council.

16. *Loyalist* (Aug. 1993), 6.

17. The material in this section comes from my book *God Save Ulster! The Religion and Politics of Paisleyism* (Oxford, 1986). See also C. Smyth, *Ian Paisley: Voice of Protestant Ulster* (Edinburgh, 1987), and E. Moloney and A. Pollak, *Paisley* (Swords, 1986).

18. Details of the UPV and its activities can be found in R. Boulton, *The UVF 1966–1973: An Anatomy of Loyalist Rebellion* (Dublin, 1973), which conveys some of the flavour of the times but is rather reliant on contested statements made to the police, and in Moloney and Pollak, *Paisley.*

19. Bruce, *God Save Ulster*, 249.

20. B. O'Duffy, 'Containment or Regulation? The British Approach to Ethnic Conflict in Northern Ireland', in J. McGarry, and B. O'Leary (eds.), *The Politics of Ethnic Conflict Regulation* (London, 1993), 130.

21. D. Armstrong, and H. Saunders, *A Road too Wide: The Price of Reconciliation in Northern Ireland* (Basingstoke, 1985).

22. N. Bradford, *A Sword Bathed in Heaven: The Life, Faith and Cruel Death of Robert Bradford MP* (Basingstoke, 1984).

23. On the social functions of religion as 'theodicy', see P. L. Berger, *The Sacred Canopy: Elements of a Sociological Theory of Religion* (Garden City, NY, 1967).

24. For a more detailed discussion of religion and ethnicity, see R. Wallis, S. Bruce, and D. Taylor, 'Ethnicity and Evangelicalism: Ian Paisley and Protestant Politics in Ulster', *Comparative Studies in Society and History*, 29 (1987), 293–313. On the links between Catholicism, Irish nationalism, and the development of the Irish Republic, see J. Fulton, *The Tragedy of Belief: Division, Politics and Religion in Ireland* (Oxford, 1991).

25. For general discussions of the 'secularization' thesis, see S. Bruce, (ed.), *Religion and Modernization* (Oxford, 1992).

26. The image of northern Catholics as a persecuted and impoverished minority has become so firmly established that one risks being regarded as a unionist bigot to question any aspect of it. There is not the space here to engage in detailed evaluations of claims in discrimination in the several spheres of life, but, for a well-argued unionist critique, see J. Morrison, *The Ulster Cover-up* (Lurgan, 1993). For a magisterial review of the literature, see J. Whyte, *Interpreting Northern Ireland* (Oxford, 1990).

27. My views of the genesis and nature of nationalism are those of Ernest Gellner and Anthony Smith; for an introduction to the debate, see E. Gellner, *Nations and Nationalism* (Oxford, 1986), and A. Smith, *National Identity* (Harmondsworth, Middx, 1991).

28. The proportions vary from year to year and with the structure of the surveys, but opinion polls have rarely shown more than 16% of Protestants choosing an independent Ulster as their preferred

option. Without making too much of this, it is possible to see the increase in preference for an independent Ulster as indicative of increasing Protestant despair. In 1974 surveys showed either 7% (Moxon-Browne, *Nation*, 115) or 2% of Protestants (NOP April 1974 poll for BBC Ulster) in favour of independence. A NOP poll for UTV in February 1982 gave 3% of Protestants in favour of independence, but an Ulster Marketing Services poll for *Sunday Life* in February 1989 gave 19% of Protestants saying it was acceptable. Given that the percentages can vary a great deal according to just how the question was asked, we are forced to rely rather on our intuition, and mine is that, while the number of Protestants who actually want an independent state remains small, the number who think it might be the only alternative to a united Ireland, and who are therefore reconciling themselves to it, has increased over the period of my interest in Northern Ireland. See also the data in the last paragraph of Ch. 4.

29. J. Baker, *The McMahon Family Murders and the Belfast Troubles 1920–22* (Belfast, 1993); Farrell, *Arming the Protestants*.
30. But they do their best to imply it. The UCDC had written into its constitution the rule that 'Any member associated with, or giving support to, any subversive or lawless activities whatsoever shall be expelled from the body'. Rather than see this as evidence that Paisley was always concerned to separate himself from criminals, Moloney and Pollak say 'It would prove an extremely useful rule' (*Paisley*, 123). By hinting that the rule was written in anticipation of trouble, the authors manage to suggest that Paisley was responsible for the trouble. By that logic, legislators would be responsible for law-breaking! In response to the 1993 Greysteel loyalist killings, Paisley said: 'These murders come from hell and they lead to hell' (*Independent*, 2 Nov. 1993), and he would be one of the very few people who use the word 'hell' literally.
31. D. McKittrick, *Despatches from Belfast* (Belfast, 1989), 171.
32. Ibid. 172.
33. Boulton, *The UVF*, 51.

CHAPTER 2. THE DISMAL VISION

1. *Irish News*, 1 Apr. 1993.
2. On the tripartite treaty between London, Dublin, and Belfast, see D. Harkness, *Northern Ireland since 1920* (Dublin, 1983), 43.

3. *Irish News*, 7 July 1993.
4. Ibid.
5. C. C. O'Brien, *Passion and Cunning and other Essays* (London, 1988), 297.
6. A. O'Day, and Y. Alexander (eds), *Ireland's Terrorist Trauma: Interdisciplinary Perspectives* (Brighton, 1989), 4.
7. *Independent*, 31 Oct. 1993.
8. *Sunday Tribune*, 31 Oct. 1993.
9. *Irish News*, 26 Nov. 1993.
10. For a detailed analysis of loyalist responses to the McGurk's Bar bombing and loyalist attitudes to violence generally, see S. Bruce, 'Protestantism and Terrorism in Northern Ireland', in O'Day and Alexander (eds), *Ireland's Terrorist Trauma*, 13–33.
11. That republican violence is morally superior to loyalist killing is widely accepted by the academic left; see G. Bell, *The Protestants of Ulster* (London, 1976), and K. J. Kelley, *The Longest War* (London, 1988). A *Guardian* review of my *Red Hand* (3 Sept. 1993) pointed to my failure to contrast sectarian loyalist terror and non-sectarian republican terror as a major weakness. I do not know what one can do to disabuse the romanticizers of republican terror other than to remind the reader of examples such as the following. On 20 March 1972 the IRA planted a large car bomb in Lower Donegall Street in Belfast and then phoned in a hoax call which caused police to usher people away from the false danger area and straight into the reach of the real bomb. Six people were killed and over 100 wounded.
12. *Herald*, 27 Apr. 1993.
13. *Belfast Telegraph*, 1 May 1993.
14. *Irish News*, 16 Apr. 1993.
15. Department of Health and Social Services/Registrar General Northern Ireland, *The Northern Ireland Census 1991: Religion Report* (Belfast, 1993).
16. *Irish News*, 19 Aug. 1993.
17. Many submissions to the Opsahl Commission mentioned Protestant population decline and shift; see A. Pollak, *A Citizen's Inquiry: The Opsahl Report on Northern Ireland* (Dublin, 1993), esp. 38–42.
18. *Irish News*, 28 Jan. 1993.
19. *Belfast Telegraph*, 30 Aug. 1993. See also R. D. Osborne, R. L. Miller, R. J. Cormack, and A. P. Williamson, 'Trends in Participation in Higher Education in Northern Ireland', *Economic and Social Review*, 19 (1988), 283–301.

20. *Sunday Times*, 5 Apr. 1993. The percentages vary with the nature of the question. In some polls people are asked 'Is X acceptable or unacceptable' for each option. A 1989 *Sunday Life* poll (26 Feb.) showed the following order for acceptability to Catholics: power-sharing (57%), federal Ireland (56%), joint authority (47%), united Ireland (47%), integration with Britain (36%). A Feb. 1982 NOP poll for UTV showed similar proportions, even though the hunger-strike deaths might have been expected to have increased polarization: 62% of Catholics thought remaining part of the UK with its own assembly with guarantees for Catholics was acceptable; 58% would accept full integration with the Republic, 39% would accept integration with Britain. When asked to chose just one option, only 38% of Catholics wanted full integration with the Republic.

21. Cited in J. Morrison, *The Ulster Cover-up* (Lurgan, 1993), 80.

22. E. Moxon-Browne, *Nation, Class and Creed in Northern Ireland* (Aldershot, 1983).

23. For a recent critique of the claim that unionist-controlled councils allocated public housing in a discriminatory manner, see Morrison, *Ulster Cover-up*.

24. Figures provided by Brian Gurney of the Ulster Community Action Network (UCAN). As I have not been involved in the analysis of the original data, I cannot vouch for these figures, but to the lay reader they seem a reasonable conclusion from the reports. According to UCAN, other sources show a similar pattern of discrimination against the Protestant Waterside. In 1990–2 the International Fund for Ireland disbursed almost £8m. to projects in Derry Cityside and £52,000 to projects in the Waterside. In 1989–90 the Northern Ireland Voluntary Trust funded twenty-seven projects worth £78,000 in the Cityside and two Protestant groups to a tune of £3,150 in the Waterside. According to its 1992 report, the Community Relations Council funded eighteen projects in Derry; only one was for a Protestant group.

25. Derry SDLP politician quoted in the Opsahl report; A. Pollak, *A Citizen's Enquiry*, 41.

26. Some vestige of elected representation remains in the Northern Ireland Housing Council, which has one councillor from each of the twenty-six councils. This elects some members of the Housing Executive's Board. Unionists have regularly caucused to ensure that SDLP representatives are not elected to the Board, but then, as Progressive Unionist councillor Hughie Smyth complained, it is

twenty-one years since any Belfast councillor was elected (*Irish News*, 8 Oct. 1993). The influence of the Council on housing policy is so small that this is a dispute almost entirely about symbolism.

27. Cameron Commission, *Disturbances in Northern Ireland: Report of the Commission Appointed by the Governor of Northern Ireland* (Belfast, 1969, Cmnd. 532). For the most measured evaluations of the extent and nature of discrimination, see J. Whyte, *Interpreting Northern Ireland* (Oxford, 1990), and R. J. Cormack, and R. D. Osborne, (eds.), *Discrimination and Public Policy in Northern Ireland* (Oxford, 1991).

28. Cormack and Osborne, *Discrimination*, 16.

29. R. D. Osborne, R. J. Cormack, and A. M. Gallagher, 'Educational Qualifications and the Labour Market', in Cormack and Osborne (eds), *Discrimination*, 93–119.

30. *Irish News*, 12 May 1993.

31. See *Irish News* (16 Sept. 1993) for such a story concerning the aircraft-makers Shorts.

32. *New Ulster Defender*, 1/2 (July 1992), 10.

33. *Irish News*, 16 June 1993.

34. M. Weber, *The Protestant Ethic and the Spirit of Capitalism* (London, 1966).

35. P. L. Berger, *The Capitalist Revolution* (Aldershot, 1987), 56.

36. M. Hall, (ed.), *Life on the Interface: Report on a Conference held on 8. 10. 92 and Attended by Community Groups from the Shankill, Falls, and Springfield Roads in Belfast* (Newtownabbey, 1993), 15.

37. L. Shriver, 'Role Reversals', *Fortnight* (April 1993), 30. Dublin journalist Finton O'Toole explored Protestant deprivation in west Belfast in a lengthy article headed 'There's a perception among working-class Protestants that they have merely swopped with Catholics as the group which is marginalised and discriminated against' (*Irish Times*, 30 Nov. 1993). He reported that no children from Shankill Road schools went on to higher education in 1992. Northern Ireland still had a streamed grammar-school system. Only thirteen out of 390 children in Protestant west Belfast passed the '11+' grammar-school entry examination. Success rates for Catholic west Belfast, supposedly the epitome of urban deprivation, were almost four times as high. The article also discussed unemployment (70% of adult males in loyalist Glencairn, every bit as high as in the Catholic estates) and reported the same resentments over 'fair-employment' policy as my interviewees expressed.

38. W. D. Flackes and S. Elliott, *Northern Ireland: A Political Directory 1968–1988* (Belfast, 1989), 67. For a detailed account of the accord and responses to it, see A. Aughey, *Under Siege: Ulster Unionism and the Anglo-Irish Agreement* (Belfast, 1989).

39. *Irish News*, 5 May 1993.

40. P. Arthur, 'So Many Words; So Little Action', *Parliamentary Brief* (July 1992). For responses, see P. Bew and G. Gillespie, *Northern Ireland: A Chronology of the Troubles 1968–1993* (Dublin, 1993), 281–3. Even the SDLP's Brian Feeney thought Mayhew should be more careful: 'The danger is that he's saying different things to different people. To a European audience, he's saying we don't care about Northern Ireland but for another audience—namely unionists—he's saying don't worry. What it does is increase unionists' uncertainties' (*Irish News*, 26 Apr. 1993).

41. *Irish News*, 24 Apr. 1993.

42. *Combat* is a monthly magazine associated with the UVF. The *Burning Bush* is a monthly edited and published by the Revd Ivan Foster, FP minister of Kilskeery, County Fermanagh. It combines commentary on current events and reprints of FP sermons. Foster resigned from the DUP over its involvement in the talks.

43. *Ulster News Letter*, 12 May 1993.

44. In 1992, as one of their responses to a poor showing in Scotland, the Conservatives started to use the word 'Unionist' again in posters and literature.

45. *Irish News*, 14 July 1993. The document was authored by Kevin McNamara, Labour's Northern Ireland spokesman. John Smith, the Labour leader, had to disown it as only a discussion document. In October 1993 McNamara was again making headlines with a speech in Cork cautioning the Republic against dropping its constitutional claims to the North. Such a change would, he argued, divide nationalists and weaken the SDLP.

46. *Irish News*, 26 July 1993. This document also aligned the Labour Party with the SDLP. It argued that, if Labour recruited in the North, it would be forced either to become a unionist party or, if it adhered to a policy favouring a united Ireland, would become only the voice of nationalists, and would damage the SDLP.

47. Reporting data from a 1978 survey, Moxon-Browne (*Nation*, 7) says: ' What can be deduced . . . is that upper class Protestants are more likely to accept a British national identity; and the lower socio-economic groups are more attached to an Ulster allegiance.'

CHAPTER 3. TALKS

1. *Fortnight* (Dec. 1991), 5.
2. *Irish News*, 5 July 1991.
3. Ian Paisley, 'Opening Speech at the Brooke Talks; Stage One'.
4. W. D. Flackes, and S. Elliott, *Northern Ireland: A Political Directory 1968–1988* (Belfast, 1989), 254–7.
5. B. White, *John Hume: Statesman of the Troubles* (Belfast, 1984), 127.
6. P. Bew and G. Gillespie, *Northern Ireland: A Chronology of the Troubles 1968–1993* (Dublin, 1993), 210.
7. Ibid.
8. The following are the main points of the statement made by Hume and Adams as reported by the *Irish News* (26 Apr. 1993):

> Everyone has a solemn duty to change the political climate away from conflict and towards a process of national reconciliation which sees the peaceful accommodation of the differences between the people of Britain and Ireland and the Irish people themselves. In striving for that end, we accept that an internal settlement is not a solution because it obviously does not deal with all the relationships at the heart of the problem. We accept that the Irish people as a whole have a right to national self-determination. This is the view shared by a majority of the people of this island, though not by all its people. The exercise of self-determination is a matter for agreement between the people of Ireland. It is the search for that agreement and the means of achieving it on which we will be concentrating. . . . As leaders of our respective parties, we have told each other that we see the task of reaching agreement on a peaceful and democratic accord for all on this island as our primary challenge. We both recognise that such a new agreement is only achievable and viable if it can earn and enjoy the allegiance of the different traditions on this island, by accommodating diversity and providing for national reconciliation.

Although the document which Hume and Adams forwarded to the Dublin government remains secret, Geraldine Kennedy, the political correspondent of the *Irish Times* (28 Oct. 1993), said that it contained three points: (1) a call for a declaration that the Irish people as a whole have a right to national self-determination; (2) a recognition that unionist consent will be required for any solution;

and (3) a call for the two governments (but especially the British government) to become 'persuaders' for a united Ireland. Given that unionists are not about to consent to a united Ireland, the British government's persuasion will have to be coercion. Quite how Hume and Adams could believe that a process which amounted to the British forcing the unionists to join a united Ireland could bring 'peace within a week' is something of a mystery.

9. *Irish News*, 26 Apr. 1993.
10. *Belfast Telegraph*, 1 May 1993.
11. *Belfast Telegraph*, 21 Aug. 1993.
12. *Republican News*, 21 Nov. 1985. My attention was drawn to this source by an article in the British and Irish Communist Organization's *Northern Star* (Oct. 1993).
13. *Irish News*, 5 May 1993.
14. *Ulster News Letter*, 3 May 1993.
15. *Sunday Tribune*, 7 Nov. 1993, headline: 'SDLP, FF set for collision'. An *Independent* headline (5 Oct. 1993) used more words to make the same point: 'Hume's tactics questioned. Talks with Sinn Fein are causing concern in Dublin'.
16. *Sunday Life*, 24 Oct. 1993.
17. *Independent*, 24 Oct. 1993. The *Herald's* headline said: 'Final nail in Sinn Fein peace talks' (28 Oct. 1993).
18. *News of the World*, 24 Dec. 1993.
19. *Independent*, 6 Nov. 1993.
20. *Guardian*, 13 Nov. 1993.
21. BBC Radio 4, *Today*, 16 Nov. 1993.
22. *Guardian*, 23 Nov. 1993.
23. Mayhew's statement to the House was carried in full by all the major newspapers on 30 Nov. 1993. For a thoughtful analysis of its significance, see D. McKittrick, 'Disbelief in Britain's Words', *Independent on Sunday*, 9 Dec. 1993.
24. The McGuinness denial was reported in the *Irish News*, 30 Nov. and 3 Dec. 1993. Details of Mayhew's admission of clerical errors in the texts were reported in the *Irish News*, 2 Dec. 1993. The possibility that the differences between the British and IRA versions of the texts might be due to deliberate and politically motivated fabrication is explored by D. Grogan, 'Web of Intrigue Clouds Versions of Events about British, IRA Contacts', *Irish Times*, 1 Dec. 1993.
25. Spring's six principles were reported in the *Independent*, 29 Oct.

1993. His previous scheme was summarized as 'Eire to bypass Ulster parties' by the *Ulster News Letter*, 8 July 1993.

26. *Independent*, 7 Dec. 1993.
27. A. Rawnsley, 'Bullets before the Ballot', *Observer*, 19 Dec. 1993, 23.
28. All quotations are from the Northern Ireland Information Service press release text of the declaration.
29. Attached to the above.
30. *Irish News*, 22 Dec. 1993, headlined the story: 'SF president says he can wring more from the British'. The following day papers reported Major's refusal to be drawn into negotiation.
31. *Irish News*, 22 Dec. 1993.
32. *Irish News*, 16 Dec. 1993.
33. *Independent*, 16 Dec. 1993.
34. For a well-articulated view that the declaration will only encourage the IRA, see C. C. O'Brien, 'Quit Now We're Ahead? No Way . . .', *Independent*, 7 Jan. 1994.
35. A. Rawnsley, 'Bullets before the Ballot', *Observer*, 19 Dec. 1993, 23.
36. *Independent*, 19 Dec. 1993.
37. *Irish News*, 20 Dec. 1993.
38. The full principles issued in a press statement on 10 December were as follows.

    (1) There must be no diminution of Northern Ireland's position as an integral part of the United Kingdom whose paramount responsibility is the morale and physical well-being of all its citizens.
    (2) There must be no dilution of the democratic procedure through which the rights of self-determination of the people of Northern Ireland are guaranteed.
    (3) We defend the right of anyone or group to seek constitutional change by democratic, legitimate, and peaceful means.
    (4) We recognise and respect the rights and aspirations of all who abide by the Law regardless of religious, cultural, national or political inclinations.
    (5) We are dedicated to a written Constitution and Bill of Rights For Northern Ireland wherein would be enshrined stringent safeguards for individuals, associations and minorities.
    (6) Structures should be devised whereby elected representatives, North and South, could work together, without encroachment or

duplicity, for the economic betterment and fostering of good neighbourly relations between both parts of Ireland.

39. *Independent*, 3 Jan. 1994.

CHAPTER 4. THE LOYALIST AGENDA

1. *Shankill Bulletin*, 56 (May 1985), 5.
2. Ibid. 6.
3. S. Nelson, *Ulster's Uncertain Defenders* (Belfast, 1984).
4. *Combat*, 1/14 (1974).
5. P. O'Malley, *The Uncivil Wars: Ireland Today* (Belfast, 1983), 319.
6. Ibid. 333.
7. Ulster Loyalist Central Co-ordinating Committee untitled statement beginning 'Over the years the loyalist working class . . .'.
8. Shortly after GAA spokesmen spent considerable breath denouncing the UFF threats as 'sectarian', the RUC discovered a cache of weapons at a GAA club (*Irish News*, 20 Aug. 1993). Recently a Jesuit priest writing in the Jesuit journal *Studies* also argued that the GAA was sectarian (see *Irish News*, 31 Aug. 1993).
9. For a lengthy interview with a spokesman for the UDA, see *Irish News*, 10 June 1991.
10. *Irish News*, 5 Nov. 1993.
11. Ivan Foster questioned the wisdom of unionist leaders agreeing to the strand-2 talks when there had not been agreement on strand 1 (*Burning Bush* (July/Aug. 1992)).
12. *Independent*, 18 Aug. 1993.
13. *Irish News*, 12 Nov. 1993.
14. DUP Councillor Sammy Wilson, reported in *Irish News*, 11 Sept. 1993.
15. See D. Haughey, 'Is New Wave Unionism a Wash-Out?', *Irish News*, 11 Sept. 1993.
16. F. W. Boal, J. A. Campbell and D. N. Livingston, *Protestants and Social Change in the Belfast Area*, Report to the Economic and Social Research Council G0023/0025 (1985).

CHAPTER 5. THE POLITICS OF ETHNIC IDENTITY

1. G. Beattie, *We are the People* (London, 1992).
2. G. Bell, *The Protestants of Ulster* (London, 1976), 127.
3. McGuinness speaking at a rally to mark the eleventh anniversary of the H-Block hunger-strike, quoted in *New Ulster Defender* 1/2 (July 1992), 3.
4. The West Belfast UDA brigadier known to the media as 'Mad Dog' openly expressed that sentiment to Maggie O'Kane of the *Guardian*, whose interview with him is summarized in *Irish News*, 20 Oct. 1993.
5. J. Darby, (*Intimidation and the Control of Conflict in Northern Ireland* (Dublin, 1986)) examines in detail the movements of population in the early days of the present conflict and the myths that grew up around them. He found little evidence that intimidation was the work of outsiders.
6. *Irish News*, 21 Oct. 1993.
7. *Irish News*, 12 Oct. 1993.
8. *Irish News*, 21 Oct. 1993.
9. *Irish News*, 14 Oct. 1993.
10. A. Kerr, 'A People's Triumph of Will over Fear and Adversity', *Irish News*, 27 Jan. 1993, 9.
11. J. Whyte, *Interpreting Northern Ireland* (Oxford, 1990).
12. *Guardian*, 3 Jan. 1994. The argument between Hume and Sinn Fein–IRA is interesting. In trying to persuade the IRA that it has won its case and need not go on fighting, Hume has glossed the IRA's goal as 'removing the British influence that prevents Irish people sorting out their destiny themselves' and offered the *procedural* point that Britain has now said it will not stand in the way of a united Ireland if that is the wish of the greater number of people in Northern Ireland as meeting that goal. Hume has actually turned back on the IRA its own myth: that the only thing preventing a united Ireland is the British presence. If it is right about that, it need no longer fight, because Britain promises to withdraw its presence if there is a majority in favour of a united Ireland. However, it is obvious to me that most republicans are driven by the desire for a united Ireland, however that may be achieved, and not by the desire for an opportunity to test their political analysis against the democratic process.
13. M. Farrell, *Northern Ireland: The Orange State* (London, 1980), 81.
14. Whyte, *Interpreting Northern Ireland*, 181.

15. D. Bell, *Acts of Union: Youth Culture and Sectarianism in Northern Ireland* (London, 1990), 96.

16. A. M. Lee, 'Terrorism's Socio-Historical Contexts in Northern Ireland', *Research in Social Movements, Conflict and Change*, 5 (1983), 99–131.

17. For example, see L. O'Dowd, B. Rolston, and M. Tomlinson, *Northern Ireland: Between Civil Rights and Civil War* (London, 1980), and M. McCullough and L. O'Dowd, 'Northern Ireland: The Search for a Solution', *Social Studies Review* (Apr. 1986), 2–10.

18. Quoted in C. C. O'Brien, *States of Ireland* (London, 1974), 97.

19. T. O'Neill, *The Autobiography of Terence O'Neill: Prime Minister of Northern Ireland 1963–69* (London, 1969), 113. The case for the beneficial effects on community relations of integrated schooling is made at length in M. Fraser, *Children in Conflict* (London, 1973).

20. Central Office of Information, *Aspects of Britain: Northern Ireland* (London, 1992).

21. W. I. Thomas, *The Unadjusted Girl* (Boston, 1923).

22. D. Murray, *Worlds Apart: Segregated Schools in Northern Ireland* (Belfast, 1985).

23. M. Crozier, (ed.), *Cultural Traditions in Northern Ireland* (Belfast, 1989). The tension between the cultural-traditions attempt to rewrite present political differences as interesting but inert history and the use by present protagonists of history as legitimation is not without its ironic humour. The Ulster Society for the Promotion of Ulster-British Heritage and Culture is an Orange and Protestant body dedicated to repelling the Gaelic Irish attempts to 'dye Ulster's cultural tartan a solid emerald green' (*New Ulster*, 20 (summer 1993). It produces popular historical publications on famous Orangemen, Ulstermen who became Presidents of the United States, the Blitz in Belfast, and the like. It also organizes lectures and seminars and (the one that caught my eye) popular events such as 'A re-enactment of the Larne Gunrunning'—the famous smuggling into Ulster by the 1912 UVF of large amounts of German weapons. I read that item just after the news reports of the discovery of another boat of rifles destined for the present UVF.

24. Northern Ireland Information Service, 'Joint Statement: Anglo-Irish Intergovernmental Conference, London, 3 Feb. 1993'.

25. A. Pollak, *A Citizen's Inquiry: The Opsahl Report on Northern Ireland*, (Dublin, 1993), 21.

26. Crozier, *Cultural Traditions*, 31.

27. A. Smith, *The Ethnic Revival in the Modern World* (Cambridge, 1981), 67.
28. A. Smith, *National Identity* (Harmondsworth, Middx, 1991), 20.
29. B. Anderson, *Imagined Communities: Reflections on the Origin and Spread of Nationalism* (London, 1983).
30. Pollak, *A Citizen's Inquiry*, 112. This point was made in a critique of the Opsahl Commission by P. Emerson, 'Danger in Ignoring the Non-Sectarian Element', *Irish News*, 29 June 1993.
31. A. M. Gallagher, 'Community Relations', in P. Stringer and G. Robinson (eds.), *Social Attitudes in Northern Ireland: The Third Report* (Belfast, 1993), 37.
32. S. Bruce, *God Save Ulster! The Religion and Politics of Paisleyism* (Oxford, 1986), 268.
33. Farrell, *The Orange State*, 333–4
34. Whyte, *Interpreting Northern Ireland*, 232.
35. Ibid.
36. Des O'Malley, then leader of the Progressive Democrats, probably spoke for a lot of southerners when he said that joint responsibility would have to mean picking up half the tab and the Republic could not afford it (*Irish News*, 2 Oct. 1993). A poll in the Republic a month later showed that 75% of people would not be willing to pay higher taxes to achieve a united Ireland (*Irish Independent*, 18 Dec. 1993). When asked to chose between a united Ireland and a negotiated internal solution for Northern Ireland, only 30% chose a united Ireland. Perhaps most indicative, an *Irish Times* poll (7 Oct. 1993) showed that 57% were unhappy with the performance of the Labour–FF coalition government; only 2% were unhappy about the lack of a Northern Ireland policy, which was the same proportion who were concerned about the cost of phone calls.

Abbreviations

CLMC	Combined Loyalist Military Command
DUP	Democratic Unionist Party
FEA	Fair Employment Agency
FEC	Fair Employment Commission
FF	Fianna Fail
FP	Free Presbyterian
GAA	Gaelic Athletic Association
IRA	Irish Republican Army
NUPRG	New Ulster Political Research Group
OUP	Official Unionist Party
PAF	Protestant Action Force
PUP	Progressive Unionist Party
RHC	Red Hand Commando
RUC	Royal Ulster Constabulary
SAS	Special Air Service
SDLP	Social Democratic and Labour Party
SNP	Scottish National Party
UCAN	Ulster Community Action Network
UCDC	Ulster Constitution Defence Committee
UDA	Ulster Defence Association
UDF	Ulster Defence Force
UDP	Ulster Democratic Party
UFF	Ulster Freedom Fighters
ULDP	Ulster Loyalist Democratic Party
UPV	Ulster Protestant Volunteers
USC	Ulster Service Corps
UUP	Ulster Unionist Party
UVF	Ulster Volunteer Force
UWC	Ulster Workers' Council
UYM	Ulster Young Militants
VPP	Volunteer Political Party
VSC	Vanguard Service Corps
YVC	Young Citizens' Volunteers

Index

176 *Index*